ALEX CROPLEY played for Hibernian,
clubs, among others. Born in Aldersho
football players, he also played for the S
Two dreadful leg-breaks resulted in m
being missed before his move to Asto.. ....
'Studs' at Villa because of his ferocious tackling, Cropley retired due to
injuries during his tenure there.

TOM WRIGHT was taken to his first game aged nine, a friendly against
Leicester City at Easter Road in February 1957. Little did he realise that
football, and Hibs in particular, would become such a major influence in
his life from that day on. Wright has now been a Hibs supporter for over
50 years, and has the scars to prove it. Previously the Secretary of the Hibs
Former Players' Association, Wright is now the official club historian and
curator of the Hibernian Historical Trust. He is the author of *Hibernian:
From Joe Baker to Turnbull's Tornadoes* and *The Golden Years: Hibernian
in the Days of the Famous Five*.

CROPS
The Alex Cropley Story

ALEX CROPLEY

with

TOM WRIGHT

Luath Press Limited

EDINBURGH

www.luath.co.uk

First published 2013
New edition 2016

ISBN: 978-1-910745-73-1

The paper used in this book is recyclable. It is made from low-chlorine pulps
produced in a low-energy, low-emissions manner from renewable forests.

Printed by Bell & Bain Ltd., Glasgow

Typeset in 11 point Sabon by Main Point Books, Edinburgh

To my mum, brother Tam, my wife Elizabeth and family

Contents

Acknowledgements

I am particularly grateful to both Andy Gray and Pat Stanton for kindly agreeing to write the Foreword, and the Last Word for the book. Also for the assistance of the Arsenal Official Historian, Ian Cook, who supplied me with details of the games I played for the club, and particularly the Aston Villa fanatic Colin Abbott who couldn't be more helpful in supplying me with details from my time at Villa Park.

All the photographs in the book are from my own personal collection. Every effort has been made to locate image copyright holders and to trace sources of media quotes.

Foreword

I FIRST BECAME aware of Alex in the early '70s. I had joined Dundee United in the summer of 1973 and Alex was already impressing people with what he was doing on a football pitch. It wasn't just the wand of a left foot that he had but the way he went about his business that impressed me. He was barely nine stone, dripping wet, but feared no one. Was he too brave for his own good? He was. Did the way he launched into tackles against people twice his size cost him dearly regarding injuries? It did. But would he have changed the way he played? No, he wouldn't.

It was no surprise to anyone that an English club came calling, and what a club. The Arsenal. I'm sure he left as we all did in those days with dreams of great things to come. In the very physical league that was the English First Division it never did work out the way Alex would have wanted, and not for the first time he would miss too many games through terrible injuries.

Because of that, an up-and-coming team – Aston Villa – was able to tempt him to Villa Park. From the first day he arrived I loved him. He was even better than I thought and I very quickly found out that although our personalities were very different we shared a couple of important traits, we loved the game and we hated losing – and I loved that about him. We got very close and lived only a few hundred yards from each other so often went into training together. We enjoyed each other's company as well and often socialised together. I was also responsible for the nickname he had at Villa – Studs. I used to flinch when Studs wound up for a challenge, and he feared no one as he sometimes threw his whole body into a tackle. That meant we also spent too much time together in the treatment room.

For a man who suffered some shocking injuries, his desire to get better and slog his way through numerous recovery programmes to get fit to play again was inspirational to anyone who came into contact with him.

By the time I left the club in September 1979 we had shared some great times. The winning of the League Cup was oh so special. It was a marathon campaign where Alex played a huge part, but I think that even better than that was one Wednesday night in December 1976 at Villa Park when the mighty Liverpool rolled into town on their way to winning the Championship again. They were full of top players but we were making a bit of a stir in the league with a promising start. By the time we walked off at half time we were 5-1 up and Alex had been majestic. Apart from crashing into tackles and ruffling a few feathers, he was in magnificent form in the game. Totally dominant in the midfield with his range of passing, and when he went off just before the hour with a groin strain he received one of the biggest ovations I've ever heard.

He was eventually going to succumb to his injuries, but I've loved having Studs as a teammate, but more importantly as a friend; and the one thing I am glad about is that I have never had to feel the force of a fully committed Studs tackle. Somehow, like many before me, I think I would have come off second best.

Love you, wee man.

Andy Gray

Preface

I FIRST MET Alex Cropley over 15 years ago, when I asked him to sign a Hibs jersey that was to be auctioned at a charity event. We got on fairly well and he would regularly pop into my shop for a cuppa and a chat about football, the conversation invariably turning to Hibs.

Over the years he would recount countless stories of his time at Hibs, Arsenal and Aston Villa in front of a very enthusiastic listener. It was clear that he still retained great affection for all the clubs he had played for, and it was my idea that we should write a book about his time with some of the biggest sides in the game. The modest Alex however was unsure, convinced that no one would be interested in him after all this time. After some consideration however, and a bit of persuasion from me, he eventually agreed, and this book is the result of many meetings spanning several months.

As a keen Hibs supporter I have many fantastic memories of the great Turnbull's Tornadoes team of the early '70s in which Alex played such a prominent part. The side was packed full of incredible players and personalities, but with all due respect to the others, for me Alex stood out, his energetic and enthusiastic style of play allied to his educated left foot immediately taking the eye, and to my mind, even in the very early days, he was destined to go right to the top. Unfortunately, as good as he was, injury probably prevented us seeing him at his very best, particularly as he matured in later years. Who knows just how many international caps he would have received had it not been for this. However, it was not to be, and he retired almost obscenely prematurely in 1982, aged just 31, to run a public house in Edinburgh which was a popular meeting place with supporters before and after games at Easter Road.

Although he remains a member of the Hibernian Former Players Association, the modern game holds little appeal for Alex and today he rarely attends games at Easter Road, preferring to watch his football on TV.

Alex Cropley is genuinely one of the nicest people I have ever met. Unbelievably modest and unassuming, one would go far to find anyone who has a bad word to say about him, and I consider it a great privilege to be regarded as a friend.

Tom Wright

CHAPTER ONE

In the Beginning

HAVING SPENT MOST of my life in Edinburgh, I consider myself as Scottish as the next man but I was actually born in the army garrison town of Aldershot in the South of England on Tuesday 16 January 1951. Some people are under the impression that my dad John was in the army and serving at what was then the largest military camp in the country, but in fact he was a part-time player with the local league side Aldershot, working as a moulder in a nearby foundry during the day. Aldershot had been formed as early as 1926, but since then they had rarely risen above the lower reaches of the old Third Division South. The only exception was during the Second World War when, taking advantage of the guest regulations that allowed them to call on many of the international players who were serving at the nearby army camp, they had assembled what is considered to be their greatest side. Players included Stan Cullis, Joe Mercer, Scotland's own Tommy Walker and Tommy Lawton, the latter ending the war as the third top goal scorer in the country.

In Scotland my dad had played for the well-known juvenile side Portobello Renton before moving on to Tranent Juniors. The name juniors is actually a bit of a misnomer as it had nothing at all to do with youngsters, but was in fact a junior, or semi-professional side. At that time many top professional players would finish their career playing in the junior ranks, which by all accounts was a hard league that soon separated the men from the boys, and would have been an extremely difficult baptism for a young player who had previously been accustomed to the lesser pressures of amateur football. Apparently my dad had once played against Eddie Turnbull in 1946 when my future manager at Hibs was with Grangemouth junior side Forth Rangers.

Dad was signed for Aldershot by manager Billy McCracken in 1947 against the wishes of my grandad, a former amateur goalkeeper, who was convinced that his son was then on the verge of winning a Scottish junior cap. McCracken, a former Newcastle and Northern Ireland player, is said to have been directly responsible, because of his 'cunning tactics', for the change in the offside law in the 1920s that now required only two players to be between an opponent and the goal, instead of three as before. Ironically, McCracken would be replaced in the Aldershot hot seat in 1950 by Gordon Clark, a man who was to have a major part to play in my signing for Arsenal a few years later. There was yet another future Arsenal connection at Aldershot at that time in trainer Wilf Dixon, who would later become coach under manager Terry Neill during my time at the north London club.

Although tall and slim, by all accounts my dad's lean physique was deceiving, and I have been told that he was an extremely hard, sometimes ruthless player, who in the words of the old saying, would 'kick his granny'. Later he would instill in my brother Tam and me that the harder you went into a tackle the less chance you had of being injured. It was advice I would often pay heed to, particularly during my professional career, sometimes to the detriment of my physical wellbeing.

Born in Lorne Street, my dad was considered to be a 'real' Leither, and he attended the local Lorne Street primary school before moving on to Bellevue secondary. In those days most ordinary people rarely travelled very far and he met and married my mother Margaret Lyle who was born in Albert Street, just a few hundred yards away. They were married soon after the war before moving south to Aldershot, and the tidy one-up one-down two bedroom council house in Aldershot that actually had its own bath, must have seemed like a million miles away from the claustrophobic, grimy and soot stained tenements of Edinburgh. It was while they were in Aldershot that my mum found that she was expecting my brother Tam, who is two years my senior. In a rush of patriotism, they were determined that their first child should be born in Scotland, and my mum returned to Edinburgh on her own to have the baby. I have been told since that when I came along a couple of years later, although they both wanted me to be born north of the border like my brother, my mother couldn't be bothered making what in those days would be a long and tiring journey home, hence my English birthright, and later at Hibs the nickname 'Sodjer', which is the Scottish derivative of Soldier.

I have very few memories of Aldershot except that we lived in a very quiet street, the one-up one-down houses all with their neat and tidy front and back gardens. My only other memory is of walking to the end of the road to meet my dad on his way back from work and being given a ride back home on the bar of his bicycle. At that time my dad worked at the nearby Farnborough air base. The base had been home to the Army Balloon Factory in the early years of the century, and it was from here that Samuel Cody famously made the first ever British aeroplane flight in 1908. No doubt my dad would have been working at the air base during September 1952 when an experimental de Havilland Sea Vixen aircraft crashed into the crowd during that years air show, killing 31 including the two crew, the horrific event captured by a newsreel camera team.

After seven years with Aldershot and 172 appearances, Dad signed for Weymouth. I don't think he cared too much playing for the Southern League side, and with the family keen to return to Scotland, we moved back to Edinburgh around 1954 when I was about three years old to live with my gran in Albert Street in the heart of the city. Albert Street was only a few hundred yards from the old boundary between Leith and Edinburgh before the two had amalgamated in 1920, and just a stone's throw from Easter Road Park, the home of Hibernian Football Club. I can still remember seeing for the first time one of the floodlights that towered over one end of the street, never dreaming for a minute that one day I would play for the club.

For me Albert Street was a completely different environment from what I had been used to, and although I was extremely shy and a newcomer from England to boot, I soon managed to make a few friends and can remember my short time there as being absolutely fabulous. Like all kids at the time we were without a care in the world, and would play from morning to night in the street, our games in those less congested times only rarely interrupted by the passing traffic.

My brother Tam and I both attended the local Leith Walk primary, the same school as my mother had attended as a child, and it was at Leith Walk that I first set my eyes on a competitive game of football. Although it was only a playground game between pupils at lunchtime, I can still vividly remember how captivated I was and can still recall that the ball was green and blue in colour. It was at that exact moment that my lifetime passion for the game was born. Although I was shy, sometimes painfully, I soon made new friends from school and we would spend all our spare time playing football in the back greens of the tenements. At that time I was never without a ball, and like many other boys, every available minute at school would be spent kicking it around the playground until one day someone smashed one of the school windows, resulting in an immediate ban by the teachers. Not to be outdone however, my mum knitted me a woollen ball, as did some of the other mothers, and we were allowed to continue with our playground passion.

After a year or so living with my gran, my family received the keys to a brand new two bedroom council house at Magdalene on the outskirts of the city, the wide open spaces a world away from the narrow confines and cobbled streets of the city centre. Magdalene was bordered by Niddrie and Bingham, and also what we considered to be the much posher Duddingston. The scheme had been built specifically to accommodate the overflow from the centre of a city that was then in the middle of a major slum clearance campaign that had seen many of the old unsanitary and often uninhabitable 19th century dwellings demolished.

For a youngster, Magdalene was a new found world of magic and excitement. The surrounding cornfields and running burns formed part of a magical playground, and as one of the first families in the scheme my new pals and I would often spend hours playing in some of the yet to be completed buildings.

Although we now lived several miles from the city centre, my brother Tam and I still attended Leith Walk school and we would catch the early morning bus along with our mother who was then working at Fleming's, a confectioner's warehouse in nearby Albert Street. Dinner, usually consisting of soup, my favourites of either mince and tatties or stovies, finished off with a pudding, would be eagerly gulped down at my gran's house before hurrying back to school to play football in the playground. With what we had just eaten it was a wonder that we could walk never mind run.

By this time I was gaining a little bit of a reputation as a good player. Some of my schoolmates had started calling me 'Cannonball Cropley', although I still don't know if they were being serious or taking the mickey, and I was usually amongst the first to be picked for our unorganised teams, either in the playground or the local park.

Although I was football mad and rarely seen without a ball, other pursuits did occasionally occupy my young life. Tam and I joined the 37th Lifeboys based in the local St Martins church in Magdalene, sadly now demolished, where we were also encouraged by our parents to attend Sunday School. Sunday School didn't last too long as it tended to interfere with our football in the local park. There were also the regular jaunts on the number 5 or 44 bus from Magdalene, we tried to avoid the number 4 as it travelled through Bingham, an area we considered to be quite rough, to either the Salon or Playhouse picture houses in Leith Walk. The Salon usually featured two cowboy pictures and loads of Walt Disney cartoons, while the Playhouse was a little more upmarket showing most of the current films of the day. After the pictures there would normally be the obligatory bag of chips soaked with brown sauce, before catching the bus home. At that young age who could have asked for better?

On Friday evenings during the summer months Tam and I would often be taken by our parents to watch the Edinburgh Monarchs racing at Old Meadowbank. When we got a little bit older we would go ourselves, often managing to sneak in without paying. Speedway had been suspended during the war, but had since re-established itself almost to its pre-war popularity and during the '50s and '60s Meadowbank was capable of attracting crowds of well over 10,000. Many would watch the races from the ramshackle grandstand that had previously been used by St Bernard's football team at the Gymnasium in Stockbridge before being taken bit by bit to Meadowbank just after the war. I eventually became so keen on the sport that in 1967, some friends and I made our way to Wembley to cheer on local rider Bernie Persson, one of the first riders from a provisional club to compete in the World Championships. Unfortunately, the Monarch's rider failed to impress, but we did get to see the famous Swedish rider Ove Fundin, the 'Flying Fox', win the World Championship for a fifth time. Fundin is still regarded by many to be the greatest rider of all time and has since had the Speedway World Cup named in his honour.

Strangely, although my dad was a keen Hibs supporter as a youngster, and living not that far from the ground, we were rarely taken to see Hibs play at Easter Road, although I can recall the time during one game my dad telling us that he knew Bobby Combe, one of the Hibs players that day. Scottish international Combe had signed for the club in 1941, the same day as the legendary Gordon Smith, becoming a mainstay in the great Hibs side of the late '40s and early '50s that was led by the fantastic Famous Five, and would go on to give the Easter Road side 15 years of sterling service. Combe had a grocers shop in Leith Walk, and whether my dad knew him personally or only as a customer I don't know.

Probably influenced by the Friday night speedway at Meadowbank, another popular pastime with many of the young lads in Magdalene at that time was cycle racing. What had originally been just a disorganised meeting of boys racing with ramshackle bikes on a bit of wasteland, some without brakes, gradually developed into a far more organised affair. One day, my brother Tam who was a really keen rider, along with some of his pals armed with shovels, dug out an actual track on some waste grassland. Later, a group of parents approached the local council who surprisingly agreed to construct a proper track, and soon we would be racing against teams from other areas, some of our bikes painted in the Monarchs' colours of blue and gold. The events eventually became so popular that on a good night they were capable of attracting a big crowd.

Although I wasn't as keen as my brother Tam I normally took part in the races, but football remained my main passion. Usually failing to take a great interest in the ongoing proceedings, I would play about with the ball that I always carried, race my four laps when required, then return to play with the ball. My brother, however, took it far more seriously than I did and on one occasion even travelled south to compete in the individual championships. I believe that there are still photographs circulating on the internet of the Magdalene track, one featuring my brother, and another of both of us racing against each other.

A defining moment in my young life was the day the teacher asked us who wanted to be in the school football team. Because there were so many volunteers, trials had to be held, but there were no nerves on my part. I had played many times with most of the others in the playground, knew I was better than most, and took selection for granted. However, I can still remember the thrill of being handed the blue and green striped jersey with a large number ten on the back before the first game for the primary school, my first ever outing in a competitive football match. I don't think we had a particularly good team although we did manage to reach the semi-finals of a cup. On the day of the game, against Drumbrae at Warriston, it seemed as though the whole of both schools had turned out to watch us, as had my mum and dad and presumably most of the other parents. For me the day would turn out to be an unmitigated disaster. Almost sick with nerves before the game, once in front of what was, as far as I was concerned, a huge and intimidating crowd, I was totally overawed and failed to do myself justice. In fact I was absolutely useless, contributing less than nothing to the proceedings, and we ended up losing 3-0. I don't know what my mum and dad really thought about coming all that way for nothing, but I can still remember them trying unsuccessfully to cheer me up all the way back to Magdalene. I must have been doing something right, however, as my name had started appearing in the local papers, but infuriatingly, they would forever be getting the spelling wrong. It would usually be Croffee, Croppy or Croply, and although it was disappointing, I consoled myself with the thought that at least I was getting noticed.

Luckily the summer holidays were just around the corner, the seven week break quickly helping to put the humiliation of the semi-final out of my mind. Although it was obviously not the case, looking back it really did seem as though it seldom rained during the summer break, and long days would be spent playing football in the park, only your stomach telling you when it was time to go home for your dinner.

All too soon the summer holidays were over and it was time to move on to secondary school. For me that meant Norton Park, which was situated only a few hundred yards from Leith Walk school and directly adjacent to the Hibs football stadium. I can still vividly remember that first day standing outside the school gates absolutely petrified, watching in horror as many of the other new starts were made to run the gauntlet of much older boys, kicked as they passed along the line. That did it for me, I was no fool and decided to stay outside the playground until the bell rang. My brother Tam was also at Norton Park at that time, but he was with his own mates and didn't seem very concerned about me, although I suppose that would be a normal reaction from someone that bit older.

I was not particularly academic and didn't care too much for lessons, although I quite enjoyed history, geography and PT, all I really cared about was football and speedway. Being so close to the Hibs ground we would regularly see many of the players including goalkeeper Willie Wilson, John McNamee, Joe Davis and Pat Stanton arriving for training. A few years later I would play alongside Stanton and Davis, but at that time while most of the other pupils were eagerly collecting the Hibs players' autographs, I was far more interested in the signatures of the speedway riders.

At Norton Park I played for the school team in the morning, sometimes for the year above if they were a man short, and the Boys' Brigade in the afternoon. The BBs played on shale pitches on the seafront alongside Musselburgh gasworks, which was not a great location for a ball player if it was very windy, but the main problem was that the set-up was very disorganised with the games few and far between. With my thirst for the game, this was not nearly good enough for me.

One day after a game I was approached by Tom Young who was on the committee of Royston Boys Club, who asked if I would like to come along to one of their Under 16's games. None of my pals were interested in coming with me so I turned him down. Tom persisted however, and I eventually agreed to join the Royston set-up. Although I was still only 14, I often found myself playing against boys much bigger and older than me, but my tenacity and hard tackling, something that had always come naturally to me, allowed me to more than hold my own. After playing for both the school and by then the Boys' Brigade, Royston was a completely different world. We would actually play with a white leather ball instead of the old worn brown one as before, and even received a cup of tea or orange at half time.

Although I had made many friends at the Boys Club in a short space of time and had enjoyed it immensely, I jumped at the chance to join St Bernard's Under 16's, probably because my brother Tam was then playing for the Under 21's side. Tam was a very good player who could well have gone much further in the game had he put his mind to it. An uncompromising hard tackling right half, I imagine that he would have been a bit like my dad in style. Although he was a bit slower than me he was as hard as nails, but I think he lacked the necessary conviction to go professional. He enjoyed many sports, particularly golf, and it was not unusual for him to play a few holes at six o'clock in the morning before spending the day at work.

At that time St Bernard's were a nursery team for Chelsea and I can still remember the pride I felt the day we got to wear the full Chelsea strip. The feeling didn't last long, however. The following week the entire kit was handed over to the Under 21's side while we were landed with the usual well-worn jerseys.

At Norton Park the school football team was run by a gym teacher called George Wood. George, a mad keen Rangers fan who was totally dedicated to football, was also a member of the Edinburgh Schools selection committee, and I think it was through him that I was picked for the Edinburgh Schools trials. Somewhat surprised to be selected, I managed to play several games for Edinburgh in the Scottish Schools Cup against the likes of East and Mid Lothian, Falkirk and Glasgow. These games often took place at senior grounds such as Tynecastle and Brockville which was quite a big thing for someone my age. In the

Edinburgh side I was selected at outside left because inside left Kenny Watson was a far better player than me. Indeed, because of my shyness and introverted nature, I thought they all were, but it was still a most enjoyable time and a great experience. The Edinburgh side at that time contained several players who would go on to sign professional forms including Watson who would captain both the Edinburgh and Scotland Schools sides before signing for Rangers, George Wood who would later sign for Hearts and Rab Kerr who had trials for Leicester City. The centre forward was another very good player who unfortunately just failed to make it, and at the time of writing Mike Riley is the chairman of the Hibs Supporters' Club at Sunnyside, who insists to this day that he would often fight my battles for me if I was being bullied by an opponent.

I knew I was a good player and at that time people were starting to talk about me. I was also beginning to come to the attention of people in the game, including some sports writers, although they would still invariably get my name wrong. I was selected for the Scottish Schools trials in a game against Glasgow at Albyn Park in Broxburn, but although I was confident enough during the 90 minutes, looking back I didn't try nearly hard enough to force myself into the game. This lack of arrogance may well have worked against me and I failed to make it to the final selection. I might be wrong, but I think that Kenny Dalglish may well have played for Glasgow that day, but at inside left they had a boy called Tommy Craig who even then looked a superb player destined for a great future in the game. The only other lad from Edinburgh as far as I recall was a boy called Brian Wilson, a left back who spent time with Chelsea, and would later train alongside me at Hibs in the evenings.

One afternoon after playing for Edinburgh Schools at Stenhousemuir I was approached by a representative from Burnley who asked if I would be interested in going down to the Midlands for a week's trial. My parents couldn't see any problems, but although I was keen, I didn't fancy a week in a strange town on my own and asked if my pal and teammate Kenny Chisholm could come down with me. This didn't seem to create any problems and Mr Sutherland, the Burnley scout, drove us both down. Unfortunately, it snowed heavily for the entire time we were there making it impossible to play any games, and most of our time was taken up playing against the ground staff in the small Turf Moor gymnasium. On the Friday evening we were taken to see Bradford Schools Under 18's take on the Scottish Schools, and we also managed to take in Burnley's home game against Nottingham Forest on the Saturday. At that time Burnley were a very good side with players of the calibre of Ralph Coates, Willie Morgan, goalkeeper Adam Blacklaw, Sammy McIllroy and Alex Elder, but I had eyes for only one. Playing for Nottingham Forest that day was the legendary former Hibs and England centre forward Joe Baker who was in a different class, at times taking on Burnley all on his own. The first player from outside the football league to be capped for the full England side, Baker had moved from Hibs to Italian side Torino in the summer of 1961. An unhappy spell in Italy saw him move to Arsenal before signing for Forest in 1965. During his four seasons at Easter Road Joe had scored 161 times in all games, including a club record of 42 league goals in a single season, and 100 before his 21st birthday. It was a quite remarkable tally, and although it had been six years since his last game for Hibs he was still a hugely revered figure in Edinburgh. That afternoon I just couldn't take my eyes off of him. He seemed to have it all: pace, aggression and skill; and I never thought for one minute that I would be lining up alongside him for Hibs in the not too distant future.

I was assured that I would be called back to Burnley for trials at a later date, but I never heard from them again. I wasn't overly concerned, however, and was just pleased to be back in Edinburgh clutching the £50 I had been given, which was a quite amazing amount of money for me, or any other 14-year-old at that time, and I went straight down to watch Tam racing at Magdalene wearing a brand new pair of 'Hipster' trousers feeling like the 'Bees Knees'. It was also around this time that I was approached by the Falkirk manager Sammy Kean who had played and coached at Hibs for many years. Newspaper reports at the time claimed somewhat prematurely that: 'Falkirk have booked the 15-year-old St Bernard's Under 16's player Alex Cropley who is reckoned to be one of the brightest young prospects in Edinburgh'. The report went on to say that: 'Hearts had watched Cropley the previous week against Uphall Saints and had made tentative enquiries only to be informed that the player was destined for Brockville'. Despite the reporters optimism, Kean, or Hearts for that matter, never contacted me again.

A short time later after a Scottish Cup semi-final between St Bernard's and Glasgow United at Albyn Park in Broxburn, I was approached by the former Scottish International Tommy Docherty, then the manager of Chelsea, who was interested in taking me down to London for trials. My dad, however, was very much against the idea. I was about to leave school and he thought it best that I had a trade. Docherty suggested that I could attend day release classes, but again my dad put his foot down thinking that I was far too young to go down to London on my own. I was in total agreement as I couldn't imagine living anywhere away from the comfort and security of home, never mind the bustling metropolis that was London.

One game that sticks in my mind from around that time is a semi-final meeting between St Bernard's Under 21's and my former side Royston in the semi-final of the local Evening News Trophy at Old Meadowbank. The game had an unfortunate start when one of the opposing players was stretchered off with a suspected broken leg after a tackle with my brother Tam. The incident put a damper on the rest of the proceedings, but we won the right to play Whitson Star in the final when scoring the only goal of the game near the end.

On the football front it all seemed to be happening for me at this particular time. Not long after arriving back from the ill-fated trip to Burnley I was approached by the Hibs scout Davie Dalziel who had played against my dad as a youngster, who asked if I would like to train with Hibs in the evenings. A few days later Stewart Tulloch who ran the St Bernard's Under 16's side took me up to see the Hibs chairman William Harrower at his office in George Street, where I was offered £15 per week wages, probably as much as my dad was taking home at that time. I later found out that most if not all of the other part-timers at Hibs were only on about £5 per week, and I was convinced that either Harrower had made a mistake, or he thought that I was the next great white hope. However, as many chairmen at that time knew very little about the game itself, I thought that the former was more likely, and I decided to keep the secret to myself.

I was now nearly 16 years of age and playing for St Bernard's on a Saturday and training at Easter Road on a Tuesday and Thursday evening under the watchful eye of Jimmy Stevenson. Stevenson had been brought to Easter Road from Dunfermline in the mid-'60s by the legendary Jock Stein as first team trainer, but after Stein's premature move to Celtic in 1965 there was no place at Parkhead for Jimmy, and he had remained at Hibs to coach the first team during the day and the youngsters in the evenings.

I left school at 15 to take up an electrical engineering apprenticeship with Dunedin Electrical, in Gorgie of all places, but in truth I hated it. I got on well enough with the boss and the other workers, but sitting at a bench all day winding wire did not appeal to me in the slightest.

By this time I had been poached by Edina Hibs Under 17's. Although the club had no official affiliation to the Hibernian professional side, Edina were sponsored by the Southern branch of the Hibs Supporters' Club and it was generally assumed that Hibs would have the first pick of any promising player.

At that time Edina Hibs were a really good side with players like John Brownlie, Willie McEwan and Phil Gordon who were all earmarked for Easter Road. Brownlie and McEwan were already on the Easter Road ground staff and I knew them slightly from training at Easter Road in the evenings. I thoroughly enjoyed playing for Edina and we had some classic games against several very good sides. I remember one game in particular at Leith Links in front of a big crowd when I received a deep cut to my lip after a particularly bad foul. As I was receiving treatment I was surprised to be approached by my dad who whispered in my ear: 'it was the number seven'. You can guess what is coming next. At the very first opportunity I managed to take my revenge on number seven with a similarly bad tackle. As I was being lectured by the referee, my opponents father came up to me and said: 'you are a far better player than that son'. It was a lesson learned. It later turned out that it had not been the number seven after all who had fouled me. My last game for Edina Hibs was an East of Scotland Cup final against the simply named Edina at Saughton Enclosure. The easy 4-1 victory was to be my swan song in the amateur ranks, although by receiving money from Hibs at that time, strictly speaking I wasn't an amateur.

In the summer of 1968, aged only 16, I was called up to Easter Road as a part-time professional. As young as I was, I was fully aware that if I wanted to make my way in the game then the hard work would start here. Luckily, hard work on the football field was something that had never bothered me.

CHAPTER TWO

The Professional Game

THE NEW SEASON couldn't come quickly enough, and apart from a two week holiday in Lorrett de Marr with a pal, the long summer days were spent struggling with a mixture of emotions that ranged between excited anticipation and nervous apprehension. The only football that I played during this time was in the traditional but disorganised Sunday afternoon games in the local Portobello Park. The games, that could range from 9-a-side to 14 and sometimes 15-a-side, were keenly anticipated by all the participants, even those who played for organised teams on a Saturday. In the winter we would use the goalposts and in the summer when they had been removed to let the grass grow, jackets on the ground would suffice. It was during these Sunday afternoon kick about's a few years before that I had first started to realise that perhaps I could play a bit. Latecomers would usually have to wait until another player turned up so that both sides would be equal, but in my case I was often told that because I was that much better than most, I would have to wait until another two players could join the opposing side.

For some reason my brother Tam and I always seemed to find ourselves on opposing sides, and rarely a Sunday would pass without us kicking lumps out of each other, real serious stuff, and every week without fail we would have to be separated, sometimes several times, by the other players who all found it highly amusing. Although he was a bit younger than the rest of us, Ralph Callaghan who would later go on to play for Hearts, Newcastle and Hibs, often took part in the games, and he told me later that for this reason alone he used to eagerly look forward to the Sunday games. The strange thing was that at the end of the proceedings Tam and I would walk home together as though nothing had happened earlier. Over the years we had some classic encounters down the park, and I well remember the occasion some time before when a man much older than the rest of us started joining in along with his son. He was a bit of a bully and soon started pushing his weight around. My dad must have heard either Tam or me complaining about it, and one Sunday afternoon completely out of the blue he stunned us by saying that he thought he would come down for a game. You could see immediately that my dad had been a good player, and midway through the game he went in for a crunching block tackle with the older man, then hit him with his shoulder as he turned smashing him to the ground. Everyone was amazed, none more than Tam and me, and that evening we gave him a little more respect than usual. He never came down again, but as far as I can remember, neither did the bully.

At that time Hibs were a reasonable side. They had ended the previous season in third place behind Celtic and Rangers to qualify for the coming seasons UEFA Cup, but behind the scenes many of the players were unsettled. Although the club would reach the League Cup final that season they would end the campaign in 12th place, their lowest position for several years. During the summer their Danish centre half John Madsen had walked out of the club to return home. Still under contract he had effectively banned himself from the game at any level. The former Rangers Scottish international Alex Scott, who had been signed the previous season from Everton, was also unhappy at losing his first team place to the rising star Peter Marinello, and Peter Cormack, perhaps Hibs' best player at that time, was desperate for a move to England after watching a succession of his teammates making the journey south in recent years. While the dressing room couldn't exactly be described as unhappy, there was certainly a degree of unrest.

Still a part-timer, one of only three on the books at that time, we usually trained in the evenings on the car park that lay directly behind the towering main terracing. My first game for Hibs was a reserve league cup tie against St Johnstone at Muirton Park in Perth on the opening day of the new season. I was now part of the reserve set-up but was still pleased to be informed by Jimmy Stevenson during training on the Thursday evening that I would be playing on the Saturday. Instructed to report to Easter Road before the game, at that time both John Brownlie and Willie McEwan had been farmed out to Pumpherston Juniors and I was a total stranger to most of the other players. In the dressing room before the game, one, who will remain anonymous, looked me up and down shaking his head before turning to trainer Jimmy Stevenson with raised eyebrows as if to say 'what the hell do we have here', a reaction naturally that did little for my already dwindling confidence. As to the game itself I started quietly but gradually gained confidence as it wore on. After one Hibs attack had broken down, the opposing right back thought he could take me on and was surprised when I dispossessed him. Taking just two steps forward, I proceeded to smash a terrific left foot drive into the corner of the net past the helpless keeper, and even though I say it myself, it was a fabulous goal. The goal gave me even more confidence and soon I started to rove inside and out, spraying telling passes and generally making a nuisance of myself. We won the game 5-1, full back Billy Simpson scoring twice, his first ever goals for Hibs after four years at the club. Although he didn't say as much, in the dressing room after the game I was aware by his demeanour that I had earned the respect of my pre-match critic, and apart from injury I would keep my place on the left wing for the rest of the season. The Hibs reserve side that day was:

ALLAN, SIMPSON AND JONES; BLACKLEY, WILKINSON AND PRINGLE; HAMILTON, O'ROURKE, NEWMAN, MCPAUL AND CROPLEY.

The reserves at that time had a very strong side, certainly by today's standards, including several who would go on to play for Scotland. Goalkeeper Thomson Allan had already played for the league side and would share the first team position that season with Hibs' other goalkeeper Willie Wilson. After a spell with Hearts he would be capped twice for Scotland in 1974 while with Dundee. Outside right: Alex Scott, brother of former Hibs player Jim, had already played 16 times for the national side while with both Rangers and Everton, and apart from myself, there was the former Gairdoch United player John Blackley who had already played a few games for the first team the previous season, and would go on to represent Scotland in the 1974 World Cup finals in Germany. Most of the other players such as Billy Simpson, Mervyn Jones, Ian Wilkinson and Johnny Hamilton, either had, or would soon, feature in the first team. Later we would be joined on occasion by Chris Shevlane, a summer signing from Celtic, goalkeeper Roy Baines, John Hazel, Colin Grant and John Murphy. Murphy was a player that I admired greatly. My brother Tam had played against him several times when John was with Carrickvale and raved about him. He had lots of strengths. Although he was not the quickest, he had skill in abundance, a good physique and a great football brain. Unfortunately, and John himself will probably be the first to agree with me, his attitude was all wrong, and after only a handful of first team games for Hibs he would soon be on his way to Morton. Perhaps it all came too soon for him, but for me anyway it was a gigantic waste of talent.

Eric Stevenson and the former Motherwell player Billy Hunter, both of whom would have the occasional game in the reserves, were two players who would have an immense influence on my career. Hunter, who had recently signed for Hibs from USA side Detroit Cougars was a great help, patiently explaining things and was a calming influence, as was Stevenson who always had time for a kind word, and their help was always greatly appreciated. I was still training in the evenings and didn't see that much of manager Bob Shankly except for the occasional hello in passing, so I was surprised to say the least when he pulled me aside one evening to tell me that he had recommended me for the Scottish Under 17's side. Unfortunately, Shankly had been informed by the selectors that I had been born in England, and that was the end of my international aspirations... or so I thought at the time.

Since leaving school I had dated a couple of girlfriends, including one that I went out with for about six months, but for me all that really mattered was football. Even after playing for the reserves on a Saturday, I used to literally plead with Jimmy Stevenson and physio Tom McNiven to let me play for the Colts on the Sunday. I just wanted to play. John Brownlie and Willie McEwan, both of whom I knew well by then, would turn out for Pumpherston Juniors on a Saturday and the Colts on a Sunday, so I was in very good company. We had a very good side including Kevin Hegarty who would soon sign for Hearts, and Davie Clarke who would later give East Fife 18 seasons of sterling service, before eventually going on to manage the club.

I was really enjoying my football now and got on really well with trainer Jimmy Stevenson, who I knew liked me. One evening after training, I happened to mention that 18-year-old Tommy Craig had just become the first teenager to be transferred for £100,000 when joining Sheffield Wednesday from Aberdeen. Stevenson, who had been lying on one of the tables in the dressing room, raised his head saying, 'don't you worry son, one day you will go for £200,000'. I just laughed, but his words were not only encouraging but greatly appreciated.

I always listened to advice, kept my head down, worked hard and became a fixture in the side although I still had a lot to learn, sometimes the hard way. I remember a game against Falkirk reserves at Brockville when my immediate opponent was constantly winding me up, and I confess that it completely put me off my game. It was yet another lesson to be learned. My only other memory of the game was going through to the toilets before the start to see a gigantic puff of smoke, that wouldn't have disgraced the Queen Mary, hovering over one of the cubicles. It turned out that it was Alex Scott having what he thought to be a crafty smoke.

I was also finding the net fairly regularly, but was still stunned to say the least when Jimmy Stevenson took me aside one evening to say that there was a slight chance that I could be playing for the first team against St Mirren at Easter Road on the Saturday. It turned out that Eric Stevenson had gone down with the flu and was a major doubt. I couldn't wait to get home to tell my mum and dad. Mum as usual was really pleased for me, while my dad who was a very quiet, sometimes dour man, who rarely gave praise or encouragement, just told me not to get excited as Stevenson would probably make it. My brother Tam just laughed, but I knew that really they were all absolutely delighted for me. My dad was a strange man in many ways. I remember when I played for the primary school he would sometimes take me to the game, tie my boots for me, then often leave without staying to watch the proceedings! Perhaps understandably, I was really nervous the night before the game finding sleep difficult, but in the morning the kick off couldn't come quickly enough. I had been instructed to report to the Nova Scotia Hotel in Great King Street in the heart of the city that had been Hibs' regular meeting place for many years. The problem was, however, that being a part-timer I didn't know quite where the hotel was. At that time there was a working man's pub called the Nova Scotia in Duke Street in Leith, but I thought that surely that couldn't be the right place. Somehow or other I managed to find my way to the hotel by bus, can you imagine any of today's players going by bus? By this time a bag of nerves, I joined the others, most of them strangers to me, for the then traditional pre-match steak. As expected Eric Stevenson failed to make it, and in the Easter Road dressing room before the game most of the older players, including John Blackley who was making his return to the first team after a long term injury, did their best to relax me. Manager Bob Shankly also had a quiet word, telling me just to go out and play my normal game and not worry; it was ok for him I thought, he wasn't playing.

By then centre half John Madsen had returned from his self-imposed exile in Denmark and the Hibs line-up that day, 1 March 1969, was:

WILSON, DUNCAN AND DAVIS; STANTON, MADSEN AND BLACKLEY; MARINELLO,

O'ROURKE, MCBRIDE, CORMACK AND CROPLEY. SUB: HUNTER.

That afternoon there was a very poor crowd of just over 7,000 inside Easter Road, including my mum, dad and brother. It was a far cry from the attendance that a good Hibs side could normally expect, but it was still the biggest crowd that I had played before, and I was almost petrified with nerves as the teams lined up in the tunnel before the game. Once on the field, however, the nerves soon disappeared. It was as if someone inside me was telling me 'it's up to you now, you have just got to do it'; and I soon settled. Joe Davis put Hibs ahead from the penalty spot after 33 minutes, but it was not until Jimmy O'Rourke scored a second after an hour that Hibs could be sure of the points against a fairly poor but stuffy Saints side. Things might well have been different. After quarter of an hour I had a great opportunity to score on my debut. Receiving a pass from Peter Cormack, I quickly sized up the situation and proceeded to round the goalkeeper only to hit the post from a narrow angle. I hit the side net with another shot, and later blasted another over the bar from close range, before Joe McBride scored again with 20 minutes remaining to give us a 3-0 win, but by all accounts I thought I had done okay. The report in the 'Pink News' after the game that evening suggested that I had given a most promising performance, but there was a far bigger compliment from Manager Bob Shankly, a man not known for giving praise lightly:

> I was satisfied with young Cropley's performance on a soft pitch, but believe me he is a far better player than he showed today. Alex is an outstanding prospect and the best of this boy is still to come.

I didn't know what the normal after match habits of the rest of the players were, but in no way did I think I was yet part of the team and there were no great celebrations on my part. I just went home for my tea as usual before going with a few friends for a quiet night at The Abercorn, a cabaret bar in Piershill, later that evening.

As expected, Eric Stevenson had recovered in time for Hibs' next game, an away fixture against Celtic, and it was back to the reserves for me. I did, however, take the opportunity to score my first senior hat-trick in the 4-2 victory over Celtic reserves in the corresponding game at Easter Road that afternoon. Having enjoyed the experience of playing in the first team, I was now desperate for more but knew that my chances were likely to be extremely limited, probably having to rely on illness or injury for my next opportunity. The chance, however, would come sooner than I thought. Just a few weeks later I was selected to replace the suspended Peter Cormack in a league game against Arbroath at Easter Road, one that would end in total humiliation for the home side. At that time Arbroath, who had been promoted only at the end of the previous season, were languishing at the foot of the table with only three victories from 26 league games although they had managed to beat Aberdeen the previous week. That should have been a warning to us. The game was watched by less than 4,000 and it was almost possible to count the crowd individually. I managed to score my first ever goal for the first team after only seven minutes, but it was a real comedy of errors, the ball hitting off both Jimmy O'Rourke and myself before crossing the line. The suspended Peter Cormack, who was watching from the bench must have been squirming in his seat as we slithered and slipped to a humiliating 2-1 home defeat by a side that had failed to win an away game all season. I can still remember spotting my next door neighbour standing on the terracing behind one of the goals, and I made sure that I avoided him for the next few weeks. It would be my last league game for the first team that season.

Because I was playing every Saturday I had very few opportunities to see the first team in action except in midweek, usually Fairs Cup games, and I would normally go along to watch, always looking to pick up a few tips. Hibs at that time had a pretty good European pedigree. Not only had they been the first ever British side to take part in the European Cup in 1955, reaching the semi-final against French team Reims, but they had famously defeated Barcelona, who at that time were possibly the best club side in the world, in the Fairs Cup in 1961. There had also been an equally famous 2-0 victory over Real Madrid in a friendly at Easter Road in 1964, and the club were normally in Europe every season.

As a schoolboy I remember going along to see Hibs playing against both Belenenses and Utrecht in 1962. My future teammate Jimmy O'Rourke made his first team debut against Utrecht as a 16-year-old, the youngest player at that time to feature in any of the three major European competitions. The game that really sticks out in my mind is the fantastic November evening at Easter Road in 1967 when the Italian club Napoli, including the legendary goalkeeper Dino Zoff, were soundly thrashed 5-0 in a Fairs Cup tie. Leading 4-1 from the first leg in Italy, Napoli considered the tie to be well and truly over and left the superstar Altafini behind in Italy. It would prove to be a monumental blunder. It was one of the greatest performances ever seen at Easter Road, and I can still remember as a 16-year-old standing on the terracing at the Dunbar end when Bobby Duncan started the rout in the first few minutes with a thunderous drive from almost 25 yards that literally flew past Zoff. It was the full back's first ever goal for Hibs and I don't know who was the more surprised, Zoff or Bobby. That was only the start before the roof fell in on the Italian side who were perhaps fortunate not to concede more, and the referee's final whistle couldn't come quickly enough for them. Unfortunately, Bobby Duncan would suffer a bad leg break a few months later in a game against Celtic. Tipped at the time for international honours, the injury would seriously handicap his progress and he was possibly never the same player afterwards.

During my first season at the club Hibs managed to reach the third round of the Fairs Cup only to go out to German side Hamburg on the recently introduced away goals ruling. Hibs were trailing 1-0 from the first leg in Germany, but a 2-1 win for the home side at Easter Road allowed the visitors, including the famous Uwe Seeler and Willi Schultz to proceed into the quarter finals on the new ruling. All the players knew it, the fans knew it, everybody inside the ground knew it, except for the referee who was about to play 30 minutes extra time until he was informed by a red faced linesman that the tie was over. Both Hibs' goals that evening had been scored by the vastly experienced Joe McBride. Joe had joined the club from Celtic only a few weeks before as a direct replacement for Colin Stein who had been transferred to Rangers in the first £100,000 transfer deal between two Scottish clubs. Man of many clubs, McBride had been an integral member of the great Celtic side that won the European Cup in 1967, but unfortunately a cartilage operation at the turn of the year prevented him from taking part in the momentous occasion in Lisbon when the Glasgow side became the first British side to win the coveted trophy. After recovering from injury he found difficulty in re-establishing himself in the first team and jumped at the chance to kick start his career with Hibs. McBride would prove to be the bargain of the season, the former Celtic player ending the campaign having scored more goals for his new club than Stein at Ibrox. An extremely experienced campaigner, Joe knew all the tricks. Great in the air and strong on the ground, he was an incredible penalty box player and I would learn a lot from him during the next few seasons.

For Hibs the season wasn't quite over. Only a few weeks before the end of the campaign they suffered a humiliating 6-2 defeat at the hands of Celtic in the League Cup final at Hampden as I watched from the stand. The final had been postponed due to a serious fire at Hampden earlier in the season, unfortunately at a time when Hibs were going well. To be fair, Celtic were among the best teams in Europe at that time, and few sides would have lived with them on their performance that afternoon. Even so this could be no excuse for one of the heaviest defeats ever in a League Cup final and I remember the players trooping from the field at full time with their heads hung low in abject embarrassment. Willie Hunter, a substitute that day, later threw his losers medal into the sea.

For me personally it had been a good season. Not only had I established myself in the reserves, ending the campaign as the side's top goal scorer with 13 goals in all games, but I had made a breakthrough into the first team, albeit only due to circumstances. Even in the reserve games the fans had seemed to take to me, possibly appreciating my general enthusiasm and attitude. My all action style and tenacious tackling came naturally to me and the supporters seemed to approve. I was happy with my game although I was still rather naive, playing mainly by instinct, but with the help of several experienced players at the club such as Eric Stevenson, Willie Hunter and Alan McGraw I was learning fast.

It had been a transitional season for Hibs in many ways with many comings and goings, and as a part-timer I often found it difficult to keep up with things. At the end of the season the experienced Willie Wilson, Pat Quinn, Alan Cousin, and Alan McGraw were all released. I was very sorry to see Alan McGraw go as I liked him a great deal. I had occasionally played alongside him in the reserves and he was another who was always ready to offer a kindly word of advice and encouragement to a younger player.

CHAPTER THREE

Willie MacFarlane
and Turning Full-Time

IN DIRECT CONTRAST to the previous close season when I had been badly affected by nerves at just the thought of joining a professional club, I was now eagerly looking forward to the 1969–70 campaign. Although I was still very quiet and shy off the field, particularly in the dressing room, I now had a greater belief in myself as a player and was looking forward immensely to the possibility of establishing myself in the first team during the coming term, although at that particular time I didn't see this as an immediate priority. However, I was soon to be involved in an unfortunate mishap that could well have had serious consequences regarding my progress at Easter Road. Although it was strictly forbidden by the club, I still continued to take part in the bounce games in the local park with my pals during the summer. In one of the games I was tackled by my brother Tam. This time there was nothing sinister, merely an innocuous coming together, me getting to the ball slightly before him, but I felt my left knee go. There was no real pain, just stiffness, but on reporting to Easter Road I was not happy at having to tell the Hibs physio Tom McNiven the lie that I had fallen down the stairs in the house. The injury was eventually diagnosed as a torn cartilage serious enough to require an operation, and the procedure was carried out by the Hibs director Sir John Bruce at the Royal Infirmary. The setback would keep me out of football for a couple of months, but fortunately for me I had recovered in time for the start of the new season.

The new campaign had started badly for the first team, managing to win only two of the six League Cup section games, but things were about to get much worse. On the opening day of the league season Hibs travelled through to face the newly promoted Ayr United who were then managed by the former Hibs player Ally Macleod. A truly dreadful performance by the visitors that totally lacked the spirit and determination of the home side saw them surrender meekly against a team that had been forced to play with ten men for most of the game. Afterwards in the dressing room even the Hibs players were forced to admit that the 3-0 defeat had been the teams worst performance for many years. One newspaper reporter went even further, suggesting that had it been a military court of law, then the players would have been found guilty of desertion in the face of the enemy.

The following Wednesday two goals by Peter Cormack restored a modicum of respectability with a 2-0 home victory over St Mirren, so it was an almighty shock to us all when immediately after the game manager Bob Shankly announced his resignation. Lamenting that there was no fun in the game anymore, it later turned out that Shankly had been disillusioned with football for some time. Unhappy at the club's policy of continually selling their best players he had actually resigned after Colin Stein move to Rangers the previous season but had been persuaded to stay, which he now admitted had been a huge mistake on his part. Shankly, brother of the then Liverpool manager Bill, was a former Falkirk centre forward and Scottish League cap. After his playing days he had spells as manager of Falkirk and Third Lanark before moving to Dundee in the late '50s, guiding the Dens Park side to their first ever league championship success in 1962. He had been recommended for the Hibs job by his great friend Jock Stein, but by all accounts the managerial styles of both men were as different as chalk and cheese. Stein had been one of the first tracksuit managers. An astute tactician, he was never happier than on the training ground with the players. By contrast Shankly, was more of a chief executive than manager. A quiet man who was rarely seen at training, I got the feeling that he never talked much about football, content to leave that side of things to Jimmy Stevenson and Tom McNiven, and I had little involvement with him except the occasional quick hello in passing. The St Mirren game also brought an end to left back Joe Davis's remarkable record of 273 consecutive games for the club since signing from Third Lanark during the 1964–65 season. Dropped for the St Mirren game, Joe would not play for the first team again and would soon be on his way to Carlisle.

It was while training in the evenings that I first came into contact with the suave John Fraser. John had been a long serving player and later captain with Hibs in the '50s and '60s before leaving to become player/manager at Stenhousemuir. Recently retired from the game, he was training at Easter Road only to keep himself fit when he was offered the job of taking the youngsters in the evenings. Within weeks his talents had been recognised and he was appointed to the position full-time. One night, John who was then known to us all as 'Bacardi', probably for obvious reasons, pulled me aside with the instructions that he was now to be addressed by his first name and not his sobriquet as before.

Another well-known figure around Easter Road at that time and one who well deserves a mention was the likeable Jimmy McColl. Jimmy, a prolific goal scorer with the club in his day, had been signed from Partick Thistle in 1922 after a successful spell with Celtic. A member of Hibs' celebrated side of the '20s, he had been at Easter Road ever since, first as trainer, then with the job of looking after the second team on a Saturday, and latterly as an odd job man. Then aged almost 80, he was a fixture at the ground, and reminded me of a miniature Clint Eastwood as he shuffled around the place with the obligatory small cigar clenched firmly between his teeth. One particular memory I have of Jimmy is one summer when he had been called upon to paint the exit steps of the terracing. The task seemed to take ages, certainly several days, and at the end he was the most suntanned person I had ever seen in my life.

It was weeks before a replacement for Shankly was announced. Advertising for an energetic and bright young man with modern ideas, the former Hibs player Willie MacFarlane was eventually revealed as the Hibs new manager. MacFarlane had been a rugged defender at Easter Road during the '50s, playing in the return leg of Hibs' inaugural European Cup tie against the German side Rot Weiss of Essen in 1955. After spells with Raith Rovers and Morton he had since gained relative success as manager of the East of Scotland sides Gala Fairydean, Eyemouth and Hawick Royal Albert, before taking over at second division Stirling Albion. My first meeting with the new manager was one Tuesday evening before training. As the rest of us were getting changed we could hear the sound of a ball being struck. Looking out we could see the drenched figure of MacFarlane in the pouring rain repeatedly thumping a ball off the retaining wall that surrounded the pitch. After introducing himself, all the young players had a bounce game on the pitch, the new manager playing a prominent part in the proceedings.

I liked Willie and got on really well with him. An effervescent character who liked a laugh, I always felt that not only did he want to be pals with the players, but also be seen as a strict disciplinarian, a combination that rarely worked. I don't know if he had a great knowledge of the tactical side of the game but he was a great motivator and was popular with the players. He also had great determination, and many a time the players would be kept waiting out on the pitch ready to start training, sometimes for 20 minutes or so while the manager and Joe McBride finished their heatedly contested game of table tennis in the dressing room, no doubt with money at stake for the winner.

MacFarlane's managerial career at Easter Road got off to a great start with a 2-0 defeat of rivals Hearts at Tynecastle with goals from Peter Cormack and Joe McBride, the victory propelling Hibs to the top of the table. I was still in the second team at that time but was at the game. At a party later that evening to celebrate the victory, MacFarlane took the opportunity to demonstrate club discipline when he informed Peter Marinello that he was being fined after being booked that afternoon. Peter was the first Hibs player to be booked that season and was not happy.

As I have already said, Willie liked a laugh but sometimes he could be irresponsible with it. One day during a pre-season tour of Germany he pressed a lump of Algipan gel up the semi-naked trainer Tom McNiven's rear end. McNiven, however, failed to find it anything but funny and was almost reduced to tears of agony as the manager nearly wet himself laughing.

Within a few months MacFarlane would make one of his best signings when he returned to his former club Stirling Albion to sign left back Erich Schaedler for around £6,000. I already knew Erich slightly as he had played with my brother Tam at Melbourne Thistle. Remarkably quick in the recovery, Erich was as tough as they came. Hard as nails, in the early days he would sometimes dive into tackles when he should have thought twice, but he soon learned. Off the pitch he was a very quiet guy and didn't mix much with the other players, usually preferring to go his own way after a game. Although he would normally turn up at the various functions, invariably he would leave early. We did have plenty of laughs with him though. During a trip to Majorca, the rest of the players lounging around the pool were amazed when Erich dived from his first floor balcony straight into the water. On the same trip several of the players, who if truth be told were slightly envious of Erich's great physique and good looks, decided to throw the sleeping Schaedler into the pool. I was asked if I wanted to take part in the prank but knowing what Erich was like, I politely declined. Eventually four of the players gingerly lifted each corner of his sun lounger before proceeding to throw both the sleeping Schaedler and the sun bed into the pool. Needless to say they quickly scampered to avoid the wrath of the by now clearly furious Schaedler. There was also the time he arrived at the ground for training in his brand new Triumph. Leaving the car at the top of the steps outside Easter Road with its sun roof down, we were going through our paces on the pitch when the skies opened and it proceeded to absolutely pour with rain. We eventually emerged to discover the inside of the car absolutely drenched, prompting the witty Pat Stanton to remark dryly: 'That's the Nazis for you'; a good-humoured reference to Erich's father who had been a prisoner of war in a camp near Peebles. If any of the young players were brave, or foolish enough to be cheeky to him during training, Erich would promptly cart them down to the boiler room and press their ears on the hot pipes. I could go on and on. He was some man, and I still miss him.

Erich made his first team debut when coming on as a second half substitute against German side Gornik in a friendly at Easter Road just before Christmas. I was watching from the stand as he demonstrated what was soon to become his legendary ferocious tackling skills when Peter Cormack was carried off injured after both Hibs men had gone for the same ball. Gornik were playing in white jerseys with blue trim that evening so there could be no mistaking Cormack's green and white jersey, but it perhaps illustrates the defender's single-minded determination to succeed.

I had now fully recovered from my cartilage operation and was again a fixture at outside left in the second team. Several of the players who had played alongside me in the reserves the previous season, Mervyn Jones, Willie McEwan, Johnny Hamilton and Peter Marinello, had all made the breakthrough into the first team by this time but this didn't bother me too much as I believed that my time would come when I was ready. A few weeks later I replaced Jimmy O'Rourke for a friendly, against Tommy Docherty's Aston Villa of all teams, at Easter Road, my first top team start of the season. Although they were then in the second division and would drop into the third at the end of the season, at that time Villa still had a very strong side that included the likes of Edinburgh lad Charlie Aitken, who was a big pal of Willie Hunter's, Bruce Rioch who like myself had been born in Aldershot and would also go on to play for Scotland, Andy Lochhead, Brian Tiler, and Willie Anderson, a former Manchester United player who at that time was predicted to be the new George Best. Little did I think then that within a few years I would be playing alongside several of them at Villa Park.

After the game it was back to the second team for me. As I say we had a very good side who were going quite well and I was still scoring goals. There were some remarkable reverses, however, including a 6-0 defeat by Aberdeen reserves at Pittodrie, one of goalkeeper Roy Baines' first games for the club. Poor Roy, had an absolute nightmare and would not have been happy at being serenaded by the Max Bygraves hit 'You Need Hands' by the rest of the players as we made our way back to Edinburgh after the game.

At the beginning of January, Peter Marinello was transferred to Arsenal for a fee around £90,000. In my opinion the move came far too early for Peter and he was not a great success in England. I had played alongside him a few times in the reserves and found him to be a cocky player who at times believed his own publicity. He had made his first team debut a couple of years earlier in a game against Raith Rovers earning rave reviews, but probably really came to prominence after scoring twice in Hibs' 3-1 defeat of Rangers a few months before his transfer. With his good looks and long flowing hair, Marinello was seen as the south's answer to George Best. Scoring on his debut against Manchester United it would be one of only three league goals he would score during his three and a half seasons at Highbury. After a move to Portsmouth, Peter would return to Scotland in the mid-'70s, and had brief periods with Motherwell and Hearts. His was probably another case of a player moving far too soon, and it was a great pity that his undoubted talent failed to reach its full potential.

MacFarlane wasted no time in replacing Marinello. A few days later he travelled through to Firhill to sign Arthur Duncan for £35,000, and who could argue that it was not money well spent. Never seen without his permanent smile, Arthur was a true gentleman both on and off the field, and was perhaps the nicest person that I ever came across in the game. A great favourite with the fans, Arthur could do no wrong as far as they were concerned, and he would end his Easter Road career having made the record number of league appearances by a Hibs player. Centre half Jim Black was already at the club having been signed from Airdrie for £30,000 at the beginning of the season, and although nobody could know it at the time, the side that would soon become famously known as Turnbull's Tornadoes was already beginning to take shape.

So far that season, except for the friendly against Aston Villa, I had not managed to figure in the first team, but I was more than happy with my game and enjoying my football immensely. The manager must also have been satisfied with my progress as he had tried on several occasions to persuade me to turn full-time. The big stumbling block was my dad who with his background in the game was well aware of the uncertainty of professional football, and wanted me to finish my apprenticeship as an electrical engineer. Reluctantly, he eventually agreed, the promise of a three-year contract with a three-year option going some way in convincing him that perhaps I was a player after all, and capable of making my way in the game. Consequently on Monday 1 March 1970 I became a full-time professional football player.

My first day as a full-timer didn't get off to the best of starts. I entered, or maybe that should be crept, into the dressing room before training with some trepidation and was soon put in my place. Finding an empty peg to hang my clothes I changed before most of the others had even arrived. After the session was over I returned to find my clothes piled unceremoniously in a heap on the floor, totally unaware that I had taken Joe McBride's usual peg. However, Joe and I would soon become good friends and the vastly experienced McBride was yet another who would be a great help in developing my game even further.

Apparently, only a few months before Willie MacFarlane had travelled to Ireland to look over the 22-year-old Des Dickson, a free scoring centre forward with Coleraine. He left thinking that Dickson was no better than they already had on the books at Easter Road, which turned out to be great news for me. Had they signed Dickson then who knows if I would have been given my chance so early... or at all.

I had featured in the first team at outside right as a replacement for the injured Eric Stevenson in a 3-1 defeat by Partick Thistle at Firhill, but was soon back to the second team again. However, after scoring five goals in the previous four games for the reserves I was selected to play alongside the unsettled Peter Cormack in a 3-3 draw with St Mirren the day after I turned full-time, this time taking the place of

John Blackley who was on Scotland duty with the Under 23's side. Scottish International Cormack had been unhappy at Easter Road for some time and was keen to try his luck in England, posting several transfer requests. Hibs obviously were in no hurry to dispense with the talents of perhaps the best player at the club, but had probably known for some time that they were fighting a losing battle to keep him. Three weeks after the St Mirren game the fiercely competitive Cormack was transferred to Nottingham Forest for a fee believed to be in the region of £80,000. He would later join Liverpool and would be named by manager Bill Shankly as one of the best players he had ever handled, which is praise indeed. Peter would return to Hibs as a player late in his career, also having a short spell as assistant manager under Alex Millar.

I scored my first goal of the season for the league side in a 2-1 home win against Kilmarnock. Early in the game I collected a great pass from Joe McBride on the right, wrong footing the Kilmarnock defence I proceeded to rifle a fierce shot past the goalkeeper from midway inside the 18-yard box. I also set up the winner for Johnny Hamilton in the very last minute with a move later reported in the newspapers as a cute head flick, and overall I had been extremely pleased with my performance. The crowd, numbering just over 7,000, were far from happy that Cormack had been just the latest of several big money transfers over the past few years and had chanted for the resignation of chairman Harrower throughout the game. The following morning, however, the newspapers were extremely kind to me with headlines such as: 'Alex makes the fans forget Cormack' and 'Cropley set for a big future'.

I was more than happy at my progress at Easter Road and eventually ended my second season as a Hibs player having scored nine goals in 32 games for the reserves, and two for the first team in ten appearances that included the game against Aston Villa and a couple against Hearts in the East of Scotland Shield. Although I was still playing mainly with my natural ability and enthusiasm, something that seemed to appeal to the fans, I had learned a lot, gained a fair bit of experience, and knew that it was now time to take a major step forward in trying to secure a regular place in the first team. I was also possibly trying too hard. One day MacFarlane took me aside to explain that I was running myself into the ground trying to do too much, advising me to concentrate my play in the opponents half where I could do the most damage. MacFarlane's own natural enthusiasm, however, could also sometimes be misplaced. One day before a full scale practice match between the first team and the reserves he demanded that we show more application. The game ended with Dennis Nelson breaking his leg and Johnny Graham ruled out of the next few games with a badly gashed shin!

With just a few games of the season left to play, and only one team from each city now allowed to enter the Fairs Cup, the fight for the remaining European place had been between ourselves and city rivals Hearts. However, the challenge of the Gorgie side had finally faltered, leaving third-placed Hibs with a guaranteed Fairs Cup place for the coming season.

CHAPTER FOUR

A European Debut
and Injury Heartache

JUST BEFORE THE start of the 1970–71 campaign the club embarked on a three game tour of Germany and Holland and I was fortunate enough to be taken along. I came on as a substitute in the final two games of the trip, a 1-1 draw with Nijmegen when I took over from Eric Stevenson, and a 3-0 victory over Maastricht when I replaced Arthur Duncan. Based at a sports centre located between Duisburg and Dusseldorf we travelled to all the games by coach. The sports centre had its own top class facilities but there was still more than enough time for us to make several trips into Dusseldorf itself and I can still remember sunning myself outside a café with a coffee in my hand thinking: this is far better than sitting at a bench in Gorgie all day winding wire.

Centre forward Jim Blair had been signed from St Mirren during the summer for £30,000, but his stay in Edinburgh would not turn out to be particularly successful. Jim had been a prolific goal scorer at Love Street with well over 60 goals in three seasons, and it was thought that he would benefit greatly from his first stint as a full-time professional. Unfortunately he would struggle to find the net during his time at Easter Road managing only five goals from a couple of dozen appearances. Jim was a lovely lad and I got on quite well with him, but quite honestly in my eyes he wasn't much of a player, and would have had great difficulty in kicking a steady backside, even with his size 13 boots. For such a big lad he wasn't all that great in the air and was somewhat cumbersome on the ground. In fairness Jim tried exceptionally hard, but it just didn't work out for him at Easter Road and he would soon return to St Mirren for a fraction of the fee paid by Hibs. At Love Street he would continue where he had left off before his move to Edinburgh, scoring goals aplenty, and I was pleased to hear that he had been transferred to English First Division side Norwich City a couple of years later. My overriding memory of Jim was during our trip to play Guimares in that years Fairs Cup when he wanted to buy a radio. An enquiry if he could receive Radio Luxembourg and the Home Services on it, left the assistant bemused and the rest of us collapsing into fits of laughter. Poor Jim just couldn't fathom out why we were all in hysterics. On another occasion during the trip Willie Hunter thought that he would take back a pair of shoes as a present for his wife Rhona. Apparently both took the same size of shoe, and once again we were helpless with laughter as we watched Willie trying on the ladies shoes in front of a bewildered shop assistant.

It had been a great tour with lots of laughs along the way, but we didn't find it quite so funny during our return journey to London. On the flight from Dusseldorf a loud bump was heard during take-off but we didn't think too much about it at the time. It later turned out that part of the tread had come off one of the tyres and as a precaution before attempting an emergency landing the pilot had been instructed to circle the airport to burn up fuel. We must have circled for nearly an hour, the pilot ordered on one occasion to fly low over the control tower to allow the staff to check the damage to the tyre, and I believe that a light aircraft had also flown underneath us to assess the situation. As you can imagine we were all scared stiff, even some of the stewardesses were crying, and Eric Stevenson, a notoriously bad flyer shouted: 'that's the last time I'm getting on a plane, from now on I'm taking the bus'; his heart felt comments doing little to calm our nerves. Instructed by the pilot to assume the emergency position for a crash landing, I remember looking across at Jim Blair and Johnny Graham sitting opposite to see that their knuckles were pure white as they held on grimly to the seat, and I'm sure that mine would have been no different. After what seemed an age we eventually landed safely a fair distance from the terminal, the plane immediately surrounded by a fleet of ambulances and fire engines. It was an extremely harrowing experience, and one that none of us would care to repeat in a hurry.

Much to my disappointment I was not selected for any of the League Cup section games as Hibs managed to qualify quite comfortably for the quarter finals from a section comprising of St Johnstone, Airdrie and

Eddie Turnbull's Aberdeen, but made my first competitive appearance of the season as a substitute against Hearts at Easter Road a couple of games later. The game turned out to be just the latest in a recent run of drab no score draws between the teams. Both sides worked hard enough with plenty of effort but the football was scrappy, and to tell the truth the game was so poor that I found it exhausting just watching much of it from the side-lines.

I was again on the substitutes bench for the first leg of the League Cup quarter finals against Rangers at Easter Road, my first top team inclusion against either of the two big Glasgow sides. Although on from the start in Hibs' 4-1 away win at Cowdenbeath the following Saturday, it still came as a major surprise to be told that I would be playing from the start in the Fairs Cup tie against Malmo at Easter Road that midweek, my first ever competitive European outing.

In truth I can remember little of the game except that they were very poor, far different from the side that would be beaten in the European Cup final by Nottingham Forest in 1979, although it has to be said that this was several years before Sweden emerged as a decent footballing nation. The game turned out to be a personal triumph for Joe McBride who scored his second European hat-trick in a Hibs jersey, his first against Lokomotive Leipzig the previous year. Joe also had a hand in two of the others – one, Jim Blair's first goal for the club. After a quiet start we eventually got into top gear, and Malmo were no match for us. The final 6-0 scoreline was Hibs' best ever in Europe up to that time, and flattered the Swedish side somewhat in the end.

It was only later in the week that we discovered that the prominent Hibs supporter Tom Hart had agreed to buy the club from Willie Harrower after clandestine negotiations had taken place in the boardroom immediately after the Malmo game. Harrower had been seen less and less at Easter Road in recent months, often not even turning up for games, and it was perhaps no surprise to those in the know that he had been prepared to sell the club. Hart, a self-made millionaire with interests in the construction industry, was a lifelong Hibs supporter and as far as the Easter Road fans were concerned there was no one better to take over the running of the club. This viewpoint was perhaps reinforced when almost 40,000 turned out to watch our next home game, a 2-0 victory over champions elect Celtic. Although he would not have known me at the time, I lived quite near to Tom Hart's house in Milton Road and often used to see him on Sunday mornings walking his Golden Labrador, the new chairman instantly recognisable by his pronounced limp, the result of a wound received in Normandy during D-Day action with the Royal Scots.

I had played from the start in the 3-0 defeat by Aberdeen at Pittodrie a few days before the return leg with Malmo and felt certain that I would be selected for the return fixture. Unfortunately, although I was part of the party that made its way to Sweden I was desperately disappointed when Johnny Graham was selected at inside left in my place. Worse still, I was not even on the bench. Eighteen-year-old Kenny Davidson who had been signed from Loanhead Mayflower only a few weeks before, scoring a hat-trick in his first game for the reserves, was a surprise inclusion in the side to face the Swedes. Not only was it Kenny's first taste of European football, it was also his first team debut. Davidson was some prospect who could really play. An extremely tricky player with a great body swerve, his slender physique was deceiving and he was adept at riding any extreme tackle. Perhaps his final ball wasn't as good as it could have been, but that could be put down to inexperience. Another very likable lad, it was a great tragedy when he later broke his leg in an accidental clash with the Celtic goalkeeper Dennis Connaghan during a reserve game at Easter Road. The injury would keep him out of the game for some time, and as far as I was concerned he was never the same player afterwards. Unable to completely re-establish himself in the first team, Kenny would later sign for Dunfermline, finishing his playing career with Meadowbank Thistle.

Against Malmo Davidson was an immediate and outstanding success, constantly proving a thorn in the side of the opposition defence. Another surprise inclusion was full back Bobby Duncan who was making only his second top team start since breaking his leg against Celtic eight months before. Duncan scored Hibs' opening goal in a 3-1 victory, his first for the club since his wonder strike past Dino Zoff in Hibs' famous 5-0 demolition of Napoli in 1967. Like Kenny Davidson later, I don't think that Bobby, who was then on the verge of international honours before his leg break, ever fully got over the injury, and to my mind he was never the same player afterwards.

In Sweden, captain Pat Stanton was the best player on the field and it was perhaps only fitting that he should score the winner late in the second half. After the game the players enjoyed a few drinks in the Casino that was located in the basement of our hotel, Chris Shevlane enjoying the occasion more than most. It is fair to say that Chris was blootered, throwing gaming chips all over the place, and by the end of the night he was so drunk that he couldn't even remember his room number. Knocking on the first door he came to, he was discovered in the morning sleeping like a baby at the foot of director Tommy Younger's bed. I don't think I have ever seen anybody looking as ill as Chris when he finally emerged for breakfast the next morning.

A few weeks after the Malmo game we travelled through to play Morton at Cappielow. It was obvious to all of us from the start that the game should never have gone ahead on the heavily waterlogged pitch. It turned out to be an absolute farce with the players of both sides slipping and sliding all over the place before it was eventually called off after just half an hour. I still don't know if there was any truth in the story, but it was rumoured that the Morton chairman Hal Stewart had persuaded the referee to start the game to avoid him having to pay any of the admission money back to fans already inside the ground. It was even worse for Erich Schaedler who had missed the team bus at Easter Road. Only just managing to catch the train to Glasgow and the connection to Greenock, he arrived at the ground only 20 minutes or so before the start, all for 33 minutes of farcical football. After the game Willie MacFarlane was highly critical of referee Jim Callaghan for even starting the game, a correct opinion as far as the players of both sides were concerned. However, the Easter Road directors immediately distanced themselves from MacFarlane's rebuke claiming that 'Hibs wished to abide by all referee's decisions at all times'. It was perhaps the first public sign that all was not well behind the scenes at Easter Road, a fact that would become even more obvious in the very near future.

It was a huge surprise to everyone at the club when the former Manchester City player Dave Ewing was unveiled as our new first team trainer. Ewing, a teammate of the former Hibs player Bobby Johnstone during City's successful FA Cup campaign in 1956, was also a friend of Tommy Younger's, and his appointment would no doubt also have come as a big surprise to Willie MacFarlane. The new trainer was a somewhat loud and brash character who's training methods comprised mostly of heavy running and other strenuous exercises, rarely with a ball, and I don't think he knew too much about the deeper aspects of the game. You could normally hear Dave before you saw him, and its perhaps fair to say that he wasn't overly popular with the players.

Victory over the Portuguese side Guimaraes by an overall 3-2 aggregate in the Fairs Cup had set up a mouth-watering third round tie with Liverpool. The Liverpool manager Bill Shankly had watched us against Rangers a few weeks before and according to him had found the occasion: 'brutal but interesting'. The game had not been for the fainthearted, and I watched from the side-lines as Hibs more than matched the usual physical approach of Rangers. Twice behind, Johnny Graham scored the winner late in the game minutes after Willie Johnstone had been sent off for punching two goal Jim Blair as Rangers lined up a defensive wall following a free kick. The goals would turn out to be the last Blair would score for the club.

A week or so before the Liverpool game I twisted my knee during a training kick about. It didn't concern me too much at the time and I travelled through to Airdrie on the Saturday. It was decided, however, not to risk an injury and I watched the match from the side-lines. In the dressing room immediately before the start there was a scare when Billy McEwan lapsed into a fit and had to be replaced in the Hibs line-up. Having played alongside him many times both for Edina and Hibs, I knew that Billy was prone to the occasional epileptic fit. The problem didn't seem to have any long-lasting effect on his career, however, and he would be somewhat of a regular in the side until the arrival of Eddie Turnbull.

Immediately after the Airdrie game Willie MacFarlane took me aside to say that I would be playing for the Colts at Dunbar the following day. If the knee stood up I would be included in the side to face Liverpool on the Wednesday, if not, an operation would possibly be needed. Not long after the start the knee gave way again and once more I was hospital bound, missing what up to then would have been by far the highlight of my career. Unbelievably, Willie MacFarlane would also miss the game. While he was with the players at their pre-match retreat in Gullane on the Tuesday evening before the game, the manager was contacted by chairman Tom Hart with the instructions that he was not to select either Joe McBride or Johnny Graham for the forthcoming game. Refusing to bow to Hart's demands, MacFarlane was asked to resign. Again he refused, and just hours before what was perhaps Hibs' biggest game for many years, MacFarlane was sacked on the spot. Even now the reasons behind the chairman's demands remain unclear but it appears obvious to me that he must have fallen out with the players for some reason or other. Joe McBride was a typical street wise, cocky and confidant Glasgow lad who always had an answer, and he may well have had a brush with the strong willed Hart. Graham was also from Glasgow and a great pal of McBride's, and he too might well have become embroiled in the disagreement.

Perhaps we will never know the circumstances behind the dispute, but regardless of the reason, neither player was selected for the game by Dave Ewing who had now been appointed manager on a full-time basis, although possibly to appease the fans McBride was listed as one of the substitutes. Behind the scenes all had not been well between the chairman and the manager for some time, and MacFarlane himself was convinced that the dispute was merely a thinly disguised attempt to force his resignation. The decision to sack the manager provoked outrage among the supporters and the press, all vehemently behind MacFarlane who they felt had left the club with his dignity intact. The *Daily Mail* was bewildered that:

> Hibs had attempted what could be seen as soccer suicide on the eve of one of the most important games in the club's history.

The *Daily Record* went further:

> Scottish soccer has seldom witnessed a sadder or more sickening scene than the self-humiliation of the once proud Hibs.

Whether the unbelievable off-field circumstances contributed to the teams downfall I don't know, but Hibs were beaten 1-0 on the night and 3-0 over both legs.

Whatever the reason, MacFarlane was gone. Dave Ewing visited me in hospital the day after the game to wish me well and to inform me that I was part of his plans, which I found reassuring, but I was to have a far greater appreciation for physio Tom McNiven who carefully nursed me through the injury. Tom had magical hands and was absolutely fabulous at massaging injuries. He was also a great believer in bandaging, a talent he had probably picked up while working in a Glasgow hospital before joining Hibs. He could spend ages, perhaps as long as 30 minutes binding an injury so that it did the work of a plaster cast but was far less restricting. Well respected in the game, McNiven was far ahead of his time, and I remember that one of the many exercises he used to aid my rehabilitation was to get me to stand behind him following in his footsteps, gradually increasing the pace without me noticing. A great man with great ideas, he was loved by all the players he came into contact with both at Hibs and Scotland. He was also a bit of a character. He thought that he could play a bit and liked to join in the games after training, but in all honesty he could be dangerous. A former junior player with Stonehouse Violet, he was sometimes like a bull in a china shop and well capable of causing more injuries than he cured. Later, Eddie Turnbull, only partly in jest, would tell us to hide Toms boots so that he couldn't join in the games.

For a third consecutive year the New Year's Day derby against Hearts ended goalless. Once again it was a very drab affair and both teams could have played all day and still not have scored. The following day at Easter Road, Hibs were attempting to secure their first double of the season in a game against Cowdenbeath but could only manage to draw two each. Still not fully recovered from the injury, I watched from the stand. Arriving home immediately after the game I was stunned to learn of the horrifying events that had taken place that afternoon at the end of the 'Old Firm' derby at Ibrox that had resulted in many deaths. The unfolding reports were truly unbelievable and I sat glued to the TV screen as every new report confirmed more and more fatalities. The entire population was stunned to eventually learn that 66 people had lost their lives just going along to watch a football match, and Bill Shankly's light hearted retort that football was far more important than death, had now been well and truly put into perspective.

During my enforced absence the first team had found goals hard to come by, a fact I can assure you that had absolutely nothing to do with my omission. In the previous nine games only five goals had been scored, the team failing completely to register in six of them, and something just had to be done. The 'something' turned out to be a master stroke with the signing of the former Hibs legend Joe Baker from Sunderland. Joe's first game back at Easter Road after an absence of ten years turned out to be an unbelievable fairy tale, as 'Roy of the Rovers' made a triumphant return to the scene of so many of his past glories. I watched from the trackside as captain for the day Baker led the side onto the field in a game against Eddie Turnbull's Aberdeen, resplendent in brand new white boots which were an unusual novelty at that time. League leaders Aberdeen had gone more than 12 games, or 1,093 minutes without conceding a goal, which was a new Scottish record, but strikes by Pat Stanton and who else but Baker, both scored within four minutes of each other in the second half, dented the Dons league title aspirations while sending the long-suffering Hibs fans into raptures of delight.

I had missed more than a dozen games since the injury, but with the help of Tom McNiven I had worked hard, and a few weeks after the victory against Aberdeen I made my long awaited return to top team action in a 1-0 win against Motherwell at Easter Road, Joe Baker somewhat predictably scoring the goal. I was on the bench at Tynecastle the following week when goals by John Hazel and Arthur Duncan gave Hibs a comfortable passage into the next round of the Scottish Cup. Arthur's goal, the winner as it would turn out, was something else. Collecting the ball just inside his opponents half he ran fully 40 yards, brushing off the attentions of several Hearts players before calmly crashing a left foot shot past the advancing Cruikshank and into the top corner of the net. The goal brought the house down, the players celebrating as much as the ecstatic Hibs fans.

In the League Cup a Jimmy O'Rourke penalty against Dundee at Dens Park gave us narrow 1-0 victory and a passage into the semi-final. Lining up at inside right to Joe Baker for the first time that afternoon, I was initially concerned that I would not be on the same wavelength as the great man, but I should not have worried. Joe made it all too easy for me with his astute reading of the game and intelligent movement. As I remember, the game was a bruising affair against a dour and rugged Dundee side and it was probably inevitable that it would take a penalty, awarded when future Hibs player George Stewart brought down Baker inside the box, to win it. The victory paired us against old adversaries Rangers in the semi-final at Hampden. In the four games leading up to the semi-final we looked anything but potential cup winners, losing all four, conceding 11 goals while scoring only five, a run of results that did nothing to bolster our confidence as we made our way through to Glasgow for the game. As expected we found Rangers to be extremely tough opponents, but we matched their physical approach all the way in a game that sometimes descended into a hacking match, on one occasion Willie Johnstone going over the ball on John Brownlie. Our own physical approach probably surprised Rangers who at times teetered on the brink of defeat, and it was only sheer determination that allowed the Glasgow side the chance of a replay. In the dressing room after the game Dave Ewing was overheard by a passing reporter describing our opponents as rubbish, and the next morning the comments were splashed all over the back pages of the papers. As can possibly be imagined the Ibrox men and their supporters were absolutely furious, but had they taken advantage of the libel laws that were in place at the time they would probably have lost the case.

Ewing's outburst did little to improve relations between the sides and probably made Rangers all the more determined in the replay. In yet another bruising encounter we were the better side for large periods of the game. Alfie Conn had opened the scoring, but I managed to cut the ball back from almost the byline for Jimmy O'Rourke to head the equaliser and we went in level at half time. We had several good chances to win the game after the break, the best of them when Johnny Graham missed the opportunity of a lifetime when he somehow managed to shoot weakly past the post after a wonderful move that had seen him evade the challenge of several Rangers defenders. Both sides had further chances to secure the victory that would take them into the cup final before Willie Henderson scored what would prove to be a winner in the latter stages.

A season that had started so promisingly for us had again ended in disappointment, Hibs finishing in 12th place, a far cry from the third of the previous term and not nearly good enough to give us qualification for next seasons Fairs Cup. As for myself, I had tasted European football and now wanted more. Overall I had been fairly happy with my contribution, but in no way was I prepared for the events that were about to unfold in the coming season.

We had been told that the club would probably be going on a summer tour of America, Canada and Bermuda, the latter destination obviously the main attraction. However, because of last minute difficulties regarding the travel arrangements to the Caribbean island, the entire trip had been cancelled, and a visit to Majorca hurriedly arranged in its place. For some reason Dave Ewing remained behind in Edinburgh while John Fraser, accompanied by the evergreen Jimmy McColl, took charge of the party for the trip to the Mediterranean island.

Early one evening a few us were taking a leisurely stroll along the promenade when we encountered, Joe 'Hardy Amies' Baker looking resplendent in a beige suit with matching pink shirt and tie. Joe was also sporting a large matching handkerchief in his breast pocket, a style that was popular at the time. We asked him where he had managed to get the handkerchief; at this the dapper Baker opened his jacket to reveal a large patch he had cut from the tail of his shirt. Needless to say that was the big talking point among the players that evening, Baker taking all the good humoured ribbing in his stride. There was another amusing occasion during the trip that involved Joe. One night several of us heard him shouting and singing loudly from the balcony of the penthouse apartment that some of the players were sharing. Found to be somewhat worse for wear, John Brownlie and myself decided to put him to bed. However, once in bed he still had one eye open and another closed and for some time we couldn't quite determine whether he was sleeping or not. It later turned out that one side of Joe's face was frozen after a bad car accident in Italy several years before, leaving one eye slightly open even when he was asleep. Joe was another great lad who liked a laugh. Unbelievably modest in spite of all that he had achieved in the game, he was immensely popular with everyone. Although he was getting on a bit he was still some player and I still clearly remember the absolutely fantastic goal he scored from a Stevenson cross in our game against the islands top team FC Majorca that simply screamed past the keeper before he could even move. It was some goal, but something that had been a regular occurrence throughout his entire career. It was during this trip that director Tommy Younger received his nickname. Younger had been an outstanding keeper for both Hibs and Scotland before moving to Leeds and Liverpool in the '50s. One day both he and fellow director Jimmy Kerr, another goalkeeper who had been a great servant for the club before and after the war, decided that they would go in goals for a bounce game. During the game Baker unleashed one of his typical unstoppable thunderbolt volleys that simply rocketed into the net, only for Younger to scream 'I got a tip to it. I got a tip to it'. From that day on Tommy would forever be known as 'Tip' by the players.

CHAPTER FIVE

Eddie Turnbull, a Scotland Call-up
and a Meeting with Sir Alex

WE HAD ALL been under the impression that Dave Ewing had signed a five year contract on joining Hibs so we were extremely surprised to learn that he had left the post only a few weeks before the start of the new season stating, perhaps diplomatically, that he was keen to return to coaching in England. Whether he was sacked or had simply resigned I still don't know, but would take a guess at the former. As usual the newspapers were full of speculation regarding his successor, some bordering on the ridiculous. I wasn't a great one for reading the newspapers anyway, so it came as something of a shock to learn that the former Hibs player Eddie Turnbull had accepted the position. Eddie, a member of Hibs' legendary Famous Five forward line, had been manager at Aberdeen for the past few years guiding the Grampian side from mid-table mediocrity to Scottish Cup winners in 1970, and to within an inch of the league title the previous season. There was general disbelief in the game that he had elected to join a club ten places below the Dons in the table. The first I knew of the appointment was while standing at a bus stop in Milton Road, when a neighbour passing on the other side of the street shouted across: 'Aye, Turnbull will sort you out now. He'll make you all jump', the news received with a mixture of both apprehension and exhilaration. I had always found Eddie Turnbull's teams difficult to play against, well organised and committed, and with players such as Bobby Clark, Davie Robb, Martin Buchan, Joe Harper, and the outstanding Stevie Murray, they played fast flowing football with a fair amount of flair. The new manager also had the reputation as a hard task master, but nevertheless most of us were looking forward to what would be a trip into the unknown.

Eddie Turnbull introduced himself to the players at Hawkhill before the first day of pre-season training, and we couldn't quite believe it when a small game was organised immediately after the exercises, something that as far as I was aware had never before happened that early in the pre-season work-up. During this game the new manager watched quietly from a distance, probably even this early assessing just who was likely to figure in his plans and who would not. His pre-season training routine, while extremely hard, was varied and interesting. Every exercise had a purpose, normally geared to a game situation, and usually involved a ball as opposed to Dave Ewing's training that had been mundane and repetitive, consisting usually only of hard running and tedious exercises.

As expected we also found the new manager to be a strict disciplinarian which in all honesty was badly needed at Easter Road at that time. Before Turnbull's arrival discipline at the club had been lax, and whilst it had not exactly been a holiday camp, we were usually allowed to do just what we liked. Before, we could go up to the office and stamp as many complimentary tickets as we wanted, and often after training several of the players would use the telephones in the press box that were still live, on some occasions even phoning as far as Australia. All that stopped after Turnbull's arrival, and it is well documented that he went ballistic before his first game, a friendly against Middlesbrough at Easter Road, when several of the players casually wandered into the ground some time after being ordered to report. Everyone concerned was left in absolutely no doubt that it was never to happen again.

His training methods, however, were revolutionary and original, and soon we all started to eagerly look forward to training. Turnbull was a fantastic and inventive coach who's training was excellent and second to none. Always varied and interesting, everything was geared to a match day situation. For the first few weeks he would often order the back four to return in the afternoons when they would repeatedly be put through exercises geared to make them all aware of each other's strengths and weaknesses, and soon they would almost be on the same telepathic wavelength. Later when he introduced the rest of the midfield and forward players against them in exercises, the back four rarely conceded a goal. There were also the small games of three against four, two against three, and various other permutations, all geared to match situations that were exhausting but enjoyable. He was also a keen advocate of fast flowing attacking football, and small games would take place when we were not allowed to pass the ball back more than twice, all the above eventually helping to turn us into an extremely well organised side. While most managers at that time, including I believe Jock Stein, favoured the use of the blackboard to explain tactics to the players, Turnbull's main asset was an ability to demonstrate concisely on the training ground exactly how things were to be done. He was also a great believer in a manoeuvre he called 'Shadows'. This involved all 11 players in their game positions going through an exercise without any opposition, the manager constantly stopping things to explain exactly where we should all be in relation to the ball at any particular time. This could go on for ages, continually stopping things until we got it just right, but all this eventually gave us a greater understanding of each other's play and helped mould us into a solid unit.

Bertie Auld had been Dave Ewing's last signing when moving from Celtic in the summer. During his debut against Middlesbrough he was quite blatantly 'done' by the rugged former Manchester United player and World Cup winner Nobby Stiles, receiving an injury later diagnosed as a broken collarbone. As he was being attended to by Tom McNiven I noticed that Bertie's eyes never left Stiles for one second. On resuming play, Auld, a very clever player who could also be absolutely filthy, soon wreaked his revenge, leaving Stiles writhing in agony on the ground, before calmly walking off to receive treatment for his injury. Stiles himself was in no condition to continue and he too was taken off to be replaced by a substitute.

Gordon Marshall had been freed at the end of the season leaving Roy Baines as the first choice keeper. Baines, however, had been injured during the pre-season training and Eddie Pryce, a summer signing from junior side Shettleston, was between the posts for most of the pre-season games. Pryce, who I thought was a bit on the small side for a goalkeeper, performed well enough, but perhaps Eddie thought that it was unfair to throw the inexperienced youngster into the fray, and the former Dunfermline, Birmingham and Scotland player Jim Herriot was signed from South African side Durban Town. The signing of the vastly experienced Herriot would prove to be a good bit of business. A great organiser with good hands, Herriot was a constant talker in organising the defence, and in a short time we would have a 'spine' right through the side, Herriot in goal, John Blackley at the back, Pat Stanton in the middle, and Baker up front where he would soon be joined by Alan Gordon. Herriot's signing had not been registered in time but the shrewd Turnbull took a chance and played the goalkeeper in our final pre-season game against York City at Bootham Crescent under the auspices of Eddie Pryce. Considering that Jim was a Scottish international it was a surprise that no one appeared to notice.

Eddie Turnbull's impact on the field was immediate. Although we always played within a system we were all allowed a certain amount of freedom, and my own game improved out of all recognition. I scored in each of the four opening League Cup ties as we qualified for the quarter finals with two games still to play, and I was really enjoying my football now, much more than before.

In the first derby of the season I scored the opening goal in Hibs 2-0 victory over Hearts at Tynecastle, Johnny Hamilton getting the other in the very last minute. The game had looked like a stalemate until, with just six minutes remaining, I received the ball on the 18-yard line. Swivelling past the Hearts centre half Alan Anderson, I hit a fierce shot from left to right past keeper Jim Cruikshank and into the roof of the net. I have to say that even I thought it was a brilliant goal and it brought the house down. After the game Turnbull took me aside to tell me that it was a great striker's goal, as all good goal scorers always knew exactly where the goal was. Hearts had now failed to beat us for eight years at Tynecastle, and had not even scored against us in the last six meetings between the sides. Although it was my first top team start against Hearts, I wasn't nearly as excited as the rest of the Edinburgh lads at the result. Pat Stanton, Jimmy O'Rourke, Kenny Davidson and Eric Stevenson were all rabid Hibs supporters and always wanted more than most to put one over their greatest rivals, but for me it was just another game, another victory, and that's all that really mattered.

Johnny Graham had not been considered part of the manager's plans and around this time he was allowed to move to Ayr United. Within a few weeks Graham would be joined in Ayrshire by my good pal Eric Stevenson. At that time Eric had personal problems and, although he was still highly rated by Turnbull who wanted him to stay, Eric decided that perhaps it would be best if he moved on. I was soaking in the bath after training one day when he popped in to tell me he was leaving, urging me to stick in as the manager fancied me. Eric had been a great help to me throughout my career, and again I appreciated the encouraging words. I have always felt that if Eddie Turnbull had arrived at Easter Road a year or so earlier he would have been a great help to 'Stevie', and may well have extended his career by a few years. As it was Eric would not be long at Ayr before hanging up his boots, in my opinion far too soon, and as far as I was concerned he was a great loss to the game.

Turnbull, however, lost no time in travelling to Fife to sign a replacement. At that time Alex Edwards was in dispute with Dunfermline. Suspended indefinitely from the game he was then working on a building site. Although it was strictly against the rules to approach a player while he was under suspension, the wily Turnbull pleaded ignorance to the situation and signed Edwards for £13,000 which was an absolute steal. The manager later received an official reprimand from the authorities but as far as we were concerned Hibs came out of the deal very much the winners. A fantastically skilful and intelligent player, Alex had great awareness, rarely gave the ball away and was a brilliant passer of the ball. Although not the quickest, he teamed up well on the right hand side with Stanton and Brownlie, while I had to put up with Arthur and Erich on the other side (only joking!). Edwards was a very humorous lad, who at times liked to give the impression that he didn't really care, but make no mistake, he did care. He could be cocky at times, but Turnbull always managed to get the better of him. Alex, or 'Mickey', would prove to be a great signing for Hibs, giving the club almost ten years' service before moving on to Arbroath for a brief spell late in his career.

I was now in my third season at Easter Road, but because of the injury I had only managed to play around 40 or so first team games, so I was absolutely flabbergasted when the manager took me aside after training one morning to tell me that Tommy Docherty had selected both Pat and me in his first Scotland squad. Rumours had been circulating for some time that I might be included in the squad, but as usual I ignored it all putting it down merely to paper talk. Tommy Docherty had just recently taken over as Scotland manager from Bobby Brown. His appointment had coincided with a new FIFA ruling that a player no longer had to play for the country of his birth but could now take advantage of his parent's birthright. Docherty's first game was against Portugal at Hampden in a European Championship qualifier, and I was absolutely elated to be selected for the squad along with Arsenal goalkeeper Bob Wilson, both of us soon to become the first English or 'foreign' born players to play for Scotland. I was playing well at the time, as was the whole Hibs team, but I put my selection for Scotland down to nothing more than a publicity stunt. Docherty had been kind enough to describe me in the newspapers as one of a breed of tremendously exciting young Scottish players, and wouldn't have any fears about playing me in his first international, adding:

> Alex is playing in a good team and has gained experience there. The natural ability this boy has is unbelievable.

He also told me that I was to go out and buy a big display cabinet as I would need them for all the caps I was sure to get. So no pressure there then! Turnbull on the other hand was quoted in the press as saying that he was not sure I was ready for international football, but he was probably only trying to keep my feet on the ground.

Scotland were well out of the running for qualification for the European Championships and I felt that Docherty was using the selection of Bob and I mainly to generate a good crowd at Hampden. I never believed for a minute that I had a chance of actually playing, and neither did my dad or brother Tam who had a 50p bet on with my mother who was convinced that I would be selected. The 50p was in a vase at the house for many years although I don't have a clue where it is now.

I travelled through to Glasgow with Pat Stanton who would be winning his tenth cap, meeting up with Prestonpans born Eddie Colquhoun on the way. As usual, I just sat quietly in a corner saying little while the two of them chatted away about the forthcoming game. After meeting the rest of the players we then moved on to Largs, but at only 19 years of age just mixing with the likes of Billy Bremner, George Graham, John O'Hare, Davie Hay, Jimmy Johnstone and Archie Gemmill was almost overpowering. All the players were friendly towards me except possibly Bremner who I found slightly aloof. Billy always looked out for himself and it was possibly this attitude that later proved to be his undoing as a manager

Docherty had sold the game well, and that evening there was well over 57,000 inside Hampden, all for a so called meaningless game. As we waited in the tunnel before the teams emerged I looked down at the famous dark blue jersey with the Scotland badge and was almost overcome with emotion, thinking that it was a long way from playing down the park at Portobello on a Sunday afternoon. As we lined up on the pitch for the national anthem it was even worse. I was almost beside myself, and I know for a fact that had they played 'Flower of Scotland' as they do now, I would have broken down completely.

As well as myself and Bob Wilson, there were also full debuts for Sandy Jardine of Rangers, Eddie Colquhoun of Sheffield United and Arsenal's George Graham. Strangely, I had no nerves before the game itself although I took a little while to get into my stride. With Bremner and Stanton immaculate in midfield, Docherty got his Scotland career off to a flying start with a 2-1 victory. I missed a great chance to open the scoring in the first few minutes when, after turning my immediate opponent inside out, my right foot shot went narrowly past the post. This boosted my confidence. The crowd seeming to appreciate my all action style, and it was a great feeling to hear them chanting my name.

I had an indirect part to play in the opening goal. Midway through the first half I was brought down inside Portugal's half. From the resultant free kick, George Graham's cross was headed on by Bremner allowing John O'Hare to nod it past the goalkeeper. I was playing with real confidence now and really should have scored with a shot that ricocheted off the keeper's legs. Portugal scored to level things with a superb free kick, only for Archie Gemmill to win the game seconds later with a controversial goal. While managing to get his head to a Colquhoun free kick Archie clashed with the goalkeeper before sending the ball into the net. However, despite furious protests by the visitors the referee – who I thought had a very poor game – allowed the goal to stand. Near the end I rushed to take a corner and was almost pushed aside by Billy Bremner who urged me to 'calm down son, we're winning'. In truth the game had flashed by and seemed to be over all too soon. The one thing I did notice about international football was that teams would allow you space until you were about 20 yards from goal, then tightly close you down.

Overall I had been pleased with my contribution. I knew that I had played well, working hard as I always did at Hibs, and everything on the night just seemed to come off for me. After the game I was warmly congratulated by Docherty, Pat Stanton and most of the other players. I also remember being congratulated by Willie Henderson of Rangers in the foyer afterwards, but in truth it all went over my head, although I have to say, for a few days I started to get ideas above my station until I was brought down to earth at training by Eddie Turnbull who kept my feet firmly on the ground.

WEDNESDAY 13 OCTOBER 1971 HAMPDEN PARK
SCOTLAND: WILSON (ARSENAL), JARDINE (RANGERS), HAY (CELTIC), STANTON (HIBERNIAN), COLQUHOUN (SHEFFIELD UNITED), JOHNSTONE (CELTIC), BREMNER (LEEDS UNITED), GRAHAM (ARSENAL), CROPLEY (HIBERNIAN), GEMMILL (DERBY COUNTY), O'HARE (DERBY COUNTY).
SUB: BUCHAN (ABERDEEN) FOR COLQUHOUN.
PORTUGAL: DAMAS, DA SILVA, CALO, RODRIGUES, CALISTO, GRACA, GONCALVES,

SIMOES, NENE, BAPTISTA AND EUSEBIO.

Having scored five goals in the previous six Hibs games at that time I was on top of the world. Although I was yet to reach my peak I really felt as though I could do it all: beat men, shoot with both feet and score goals from midfield. And if I'm honest, for a while the whole thing could well have gone to my head had it not been for Turnbull. I was also starting to receive loads of fan mail and tried to answer them all. Possibly because she had been married to a footballer and probably knew what to expect, one night some time before I was just starting to make my breakthrough into the first team, my mum had handed me a pen and paper advising me to practice writing my autograph as I would soon be getting asked for it more and more often.

Deep down I knew that I had probably played too well against Portugal to be dropped for the next game, and both Pat and I kept our place for another European Qualifier, this time against Belgium at Pittodrie a few weeks later. Bob Wilson had been replaced for this game by the home keeper Bobby Clark.

I found Belgium to be a far different proposition to Portugal, much better organised, and I had to work harder and think quicker against a very pacy and experienced right back in Georges Heylens. I sometimes found myself with my back to goal and often struggled against the defender who was a decent player. A goal by O'Hare gave Scotland a narrow 1-0 win, but a few minutes after half time I was forced to leave the field after Heylens had accidentally stood on my foot as I was turning. I was replaced by a youngster from Celtic who was winning his first full cap... I have often wondered what happened to Kenny Dalglish! For me Dalglish should have been capped long before then as he was one of the best young players in the country. Saying that, he would eventually go on to do quite nicely for himself in the game.

I watched the remainder of the match from the bench and remember running down the tunnel to ask the three times winner of the Belgian Golden Shoe, Wilfried Van Moer, for his shirt after he had been substituted. Although it hadn't really bothered me all that much before, at the after match reception I began to limp quite badly and an X-ray later revealed, long before the injury became fashionable, that I had broken a small bone in my foot called the metatarsal.

WEDNESDAY 10 NOVEMBER 1971 HAMPDEN PARK
SCOTLAND: CLARK (ABERDEEN), JARDINE (RANGERS), HAY (CELTIC), STANTON (HIBERNIAN), BUCHAN (ABERDEEN), JOHNSTONE (CELTIC), BREMNER (LEEDS UNITED), CROPLEY (HIBERNIAN), GRAY (LEEDS UNITED), MURRAY (ABERDEEN), O'HARE (DERBY

COUNTY).
SUBS: DALGLISH (CELTIC) FOR CROPLEY, J HANSON (PARTICK THISTLE) FOR
JOHNSTONE.
BELGIUM: PIOT, HEYLENS, DEWALQUE, STASSART, DOLMAINS, VAN MOER, VAN DEN
DAELE, PUIS, SEMMELING, DEVRINDT AND VAN HIMST.

The injury would keep me out of football for several weeks, and also the forthcoming game against Holland in Amsterdam, had I been selected. My performances for Scotland had already earned me great praise, with several in the media predicting a big international future, but although I was not to know it at the time, I had already played my last game for the full Scotland side.

It was suggested in the newspapers around this time that Everton were interested in signing me. One source even claimed that the Arsenal manager Bertie Mee had been about to make a bid for me when he heard that Everton were willing to let World Cup winner Alan Ball go, and turned his attentions towards Goodison to sign the World Cup winner for £240,000 instead. Because they now had money in the bank after the sale of Ball, the rumours were possibly only speculation regarding the interest from Everton, and as far as I was concerned it was only paper talk. In any case I took it all in my stride because deep down I knew that I was not yet ready to go, and would cross that bridge if and when it happened.

The injury received against Belgium kept me out of the Hibs side for over a month and I made my return in a 1-0 home win against Dundee. Turnbull's arrival had already made a huge difference, and at that time the side was going well winning five and drawing two of the previous seven matches, lay third in the table, and were attracting crowds averaging more than 17,000.

Alex Edwards chose the game against Rangers on Christmas Day to display his own inimitable talents. With 'Mickey' in top form we were so far in front that the game should have been well and truly over by half time. In the second half I missed the best chance of the match when, with the goal gaping, I blasted high over the bar. With only seconds remaining, a corner from Hibs' right seemed to be Herriot's ball all the way until the goalkeeper was impeded by Willie Johnstone, allowing Stein to score the only goal of the game from close range. Despite Herriot's furious protests the goal was allowed to stand. Once again I had found Rangers to be difficult opponents, Alex McDonald more that capable of putting it about, but contrary to what many of the older supporters still think, I always found John Greig extremely hard to play against, but fair. Greig led by example and over the years had often carried Rangers on his own. Pacey with a good football brain, Greig was dogged, never leaving you alone for a second and was an extremely difficult opponent, although I have to say that I did break his toe one day when blocking an attempted clearance. I would probably have been sent off for the tackle nowadays but back then it was an entirely different game.

We travelled to play East Fife 24 hours after what had been yet another disappointing no score draw against Hearts at Easter Road on New Years Day, the third consecutive game between the sides at Easter Road to end goalless. The 2-1 defeat at Bayview would prove to be costly. When he signed on at Easter Road, Alex Edwards had promised Eddie Turnbull that his days of indiscipline were over, but early in the second half he was sent off for retaliation after yet another bad foul by John Love, apparently a continuation of a long running vendetta between both players. 'Mickey' would later be fined £60 and receive a 'savage' eight week ban for his part in the affray.

Joe Baker had not played since being injured at the end of November, the damage serious enough to require an operation. In Joe's absence we had done quite well, winning six of the nine games with one drawn, the goals shared out among the side with even full back John Brownlie managing to get in on the act, but Turnbull still felt that we needed a natural goal scorer. With this in mind he travelled to Tayside to sign the former Hearts centre forward Alan Gordon from Dundee United for a fee of around £12,000, which was a fantastic bit of business, and its reported that the United manager Jim McLean later felt that he had been 'done' over the deal. Making his debut for Hearts as a 17-year-old Heriots schoolboy in 1961, Gordon had developed into a prolific goal scorer, perhaps just what we needed at the time, and he would turn out to be the final piece in the makeup of what would soon become a legendary side.

I knew Alan from Jingling Geordies, a pub in Lawnmarket Close that was a popular meeting place for some of the players from both Hibs and United after games. The highly intelligent Gordon was a real gentleman, and our usual pre-training greeting of 'Aw right Alan' would invariably be met with a polite 'Good Morning'. Although he was a good mixer who enjoyed a laugh as much as the rest of us, Alan liked nothing better on our trips abroad than to sit on his own with a glass of lager in one hand and a cigar in the other just watching the world go by.

Gordon would provide us with a great aerial threat and goals by the sackfull. One of the best players I have ever witnessed in the air, and highly intelligent on the ground, he knew the game and had great movement in the box. If we were ever in trouble we would just get the ball over into the goalmouth and Alan would be lurking about.

At the end of January I was selected for the Scottish Under 23's side to face Wales at Pittodrie, my first international call-up since the Belgium game. I remember thinking that it was strange to be capped for the Under 23's side after having played for the full side instead of the other way round, but I was not complaining as it is always a great honour to represent your country regardless of the level. The only memory I have of the game itself, a 2-0 victory for Scotland, was one of their players approaching me during the second half to ask if he could have my jersey after the game.

Hibs' annual pilgrimage for the Scottish Cup got off to a great start with a 2-0 victory over Partick Thistle in the first round at Firhill, both Alan Gordon and Erich Schaedler scoring their first goals for the club against very stuffy opponents. Erich's goal was an absolute beauty. Taking a throw-in midway inside the Thistle half, his throw found Gordon who nodded it straight back. Meeting the ball on the volley, Erich's tremendous drive flashed past Alan Rough from all of 25 yards before the keeper could even move.

One of Eddie Turnbull's priorities had been to reintroduce the Annual Dinner Dance held at the North British Hotel on Princes Street. It had been Harry Swan's idea in the 1940s to help promote team spirit in the camp, and the evening in question proved a great success. All the staff were there from the first team down to the tea lady, as well as many distinguished guests including the Lord Provost. As usual Tom Hart had spared no expense and every guest found a small carriage clock at their place at the dinner table. Like Harrower before him, I rarely had anything to do with the chairman, or any of the other directors for that matter, except perhaps a nod in passing. Hart rarely, if ever, visited the dressing room on a match day, something that would not have been tolerated by Eddie Turnbull anyway, unlike during a game against Aberdeen at Pittodrie some time before when Willie MacFarlane was manager. At that time we were on £30 a man bonus to beat the Dons and were surprised when chairman Harrower barged into the dressing room at half time to tell us that we would now be on £70 if we won. Needless to say we lost 3-0. As I've said,

Turnbull hated interruptions in the dressing room, and I remember the time when the club doctor burst in during a game against Falkirk, again at half time, to tell us the unbelievable news that underdogs Partick Thistle were beating Celtic 4-0 in that years League Cup final at Hampden. As you can expect Eddie went completely berserk at the intrusion with language that could not possibly be repeated here.

In mid-February Joe Baker made his long awaited return from injury when he was named as substitute in a league game against Falkirk at Brockville. Joe had undergone an operation just before the turn of the year to remove a calcified bone that had grown through his muscle, and his return was a welcome boost. Hundreds of fans were still outside the ground when Johnny Hamilton opened the scoring after just ten seconds. It was one of the quickest goals ever scored in Scotland, but apparently some way behind the goal scored by Willie Sharp of Partick Thistle against Queen of the South in 1947 after only seven seconds. Midway through the first half I collected a ball just outside the Falkirk penalty area when I was tackled firmly from behind by the Falkirk centre forward Alex Ferguson and felt my ankle go. I am often asked if I thought it was a bad tackle, but what is a bad tackle? The Hibs supporters behind that goal were absolutely incensed and as far as I'm aware Ferguson was not even warned by the referee who merely awarded Hibs a free kick that was quickly taken. As play raged up the other end of the park the referee repeatedly gestured for me to get up. I attempted to walk to the side-lines but the pain was unbearable and I ended up being carried off on a stretcher. To make matters worse, I was spat on by a supporter as I was being carried down the tunnel. In the dressing room I was in absolute agony. The Hibs director Sir John Bruce was of the opinion that it might be just ligament trouble and strapped the ankle. Back in Edinburgh I had great difficulty in driving as I could not put any weight on the clutch, and it was an almighty relief when I somehow made it back home. During the night the pain was unrelenting, even the weight of the bedclothes unbearable, and it was obvious that something was seriously wrong. In the morning my dad had to give me a fireman's lift downstairs to the car before driving me to the Royal Infirmary. At the hospital X-rays confirmed that my left ankle was broken. I was operated on the next day when a screw was inserted into the ankle, and would not play again that season. As I have said, I don't know if it was a bad tackle or not, but in later years Eddie Turnbull told me that he had been disgusted at the challenge and would not have wished to speak to Ferguson again. We eventually managed to win 3-2 and I am told that substitute Joe Baker scored a real 'Roy of the Rovers' goal when throwing himself horizontally to head the winner from an Alan Gordon cross late in the game. By that time, Alex Ferguson, who could be a troublesome and awkward player with not much skill, and a real nightmare to play against, had already been sent off after yet another rash tackle that had incensed the angry Hibs supporters even more, this time on Schaedler.

I had accepted my earlier cartilage problems as routine injuries that football players sometimes get. But this time it was different, particularly after hearing that they had inserted a screw in the ankle, and I nearly passed out after later seeing blood seeping through the plaster. Now I had serious concerns that at just 20 years of age my career could well be over almost before it had begun.

The biggest enemy in recovering from a serious injury is boredom. Weeks of inactivity before the plaster was removed were followed by weeks and weeks of gentle exercises gradually increasing in tempo. Once again Tom McNiven came into his own, carefully nurturing me through what was a difficult and trying period. Tom would gradually build up the thigh and calf muscles with daily massages and gentle walks as I literally had to learn to run again. At times I would be champing at the bit to get back to full fitness, the boss also keen to have me back as soon as possible, but to give Tom his due he erred on the side of caution. He was some man, and every week he would know exactly at just what stage I should be at on the road to recovery, and even all these years later I still can't thank him enough.

For me the season was over, but the team was still going well. Alan Gordon was contributing a fair number of goals as were Joe Baker and Jimmy O'Rourke with others coming from all over the pitch.

In my absence a 2-0 victory over Aberdeen in the third round of the Scottish Cup had set up yet another meeting with Rangers in the semi-final at Hampden. Once again a replay on the Monday night was required, but this time goals from Pat Stanton and Alex Edwards gave Hibs a 2-0 victory in a very much one sided game, and a passage through to meet Celtic in the final.

Three days after the semi-final I travelled through to watch the boys play Rangers at Ibrox in the league. Considering that the game was between the then Cup Winners' Cup finalists, and the Scottish Cup finalists, to describe a crowd of just under 9,000 inside a stadium capable of holding more than 100,000, as disappointing, would be an understatement of world class proportion. With 16-year-old Alex

McGhee making his debut, a penalty converted by Jimmy O'Rourke and a rare goal from Bertie Auld, his last as it would turn out in top class football after a career spanning 17 years, were enough to give us a 2-1 victory.

On the very eve of the cup final we were all stunned at the shock announcement that Joe Baker had been released. As well as his undoubted skill, Joe had relied heavily on his speed, and it seemed to me that he was not the same player after the latest operation, an opinion that was shared by the manager. Joe would end his career with Raith Rovers a couple of years later, but was always resentful at Turnbull's decision to free him, and it's no secret that the pair were not the best of friends in later years.

As for the final itself, there's not much that can be said. At that time Celtic were one of the best sides in Europe, but that can be no excuse for the heavy 6-1 defeat. Centre half Billy McNeil was always a big threat at set pieces, and the last instruction Turnbull had given the players immediately before leaving the dressing room was to instruct Alan Gordon to pick up McNeil at free kicks and corners. Alan was possibly the only player in Scotland at that time who was able to combat McNeil's threat in the air, but inside the first few minutes he failed to track the Celtic defender who had the easiest of chances to open the scoring. Hibs did manage to claw a goal back a few minutes later when Gordon beat goalkeeper Evans to the ball, but another goal before half time allowed Celtic to go in at the interval 2-1 ahead. Celtic scored again shortly after the restart but in no way were Hibs out of it, constantly troubling the hoops rear guard, and another three goals in the final 15 minutes probably flattered Celtic somewhat. Regardless, it was the heaviest Scottish Cup final defeat of the century, the three goals scored by Celtic's Dixie Deans the first hat-trick to be scored in a Scottish Cup final since 1904, and it was a huge embarrassment, not only for the manager and players but also for the supporters and everyone connected with the club.

I was in the dressing room after the game to see an obviously extremely distressed John Blackley throw his loser's medal the length of the room. Turnbull, who would also have been bitterly disappointed on a personal level, surprised the players by urging them to get their heads up with the words: 'we'll be back and next time we'll beat them!' Needless to say the post-match meal at the North British Hotel was a subdued affair and did not start to liven up until around 11 o'clock. The players, however, were surprised when the manager instructed them to report to the ground during the week with their luggage and passports ready as the club were taking them on holiday. Turning to me he barked: 'This means you too, Cropley'. While pleased at having been included, I have always felt that he could have broken the news in a nicer way, but I suppose that was just Eddie.

CHAPTER SIX

Turnbull's Tornadoes

THE HOLIDAY TURNED out to be a fantastic 13 day trip to San Remo in Northern Italy, only a short distance away from the millionaires' playground of Cannes on the French Riviera. The area had once been a popular destination for the legendary Hibs player Gordon Smith in the 1950s, and it turned out to be a fabulous experience for a wee boy from Magdalene. The trip was purely a holiday as a reward for the season just ended and there were no games, just the opportunity to see how the other half lived. We arrived at our hotel in San Remo resplendent in our new club blazers featuring the club badge, all of us feeling like a million dollars, but as we were leaving the coach I overheard an old American couple saying to each other: 'Oh that must be the band arriving'. During a day visit to Cannes we stopped off for lunch at the Metropole Hotel. This was during the world famous film festival and we later found out that the famous film actress Claudia Cardinele was also staying at the hotel while we were there. A group of us including young Alec McGhee, decided to take a walk along the beach where we were surprised to be confronted by row upon row of topless beauties. This was not exactly a sight that we were used to seeing on Portobello Beach, and being the healthy fresh air fiends that we were, we must have walked well over a mile taking in the sights.

The hotel shop at San Remo sold these big cheap cigars, and one afternoon some of us bought one to smoke in the taxi on the way to having a few drinks in town. There we were, dressed to the nines and lounging in the back of the cab puffing away, when we spotted the directors Tommy Younger, Jimmy Kerr and John Christie, having a gentle jog along the beach in their shorts and singlet's. We all burst into fits of laughter when Pat Stanton with his typical dry humour quipped: 'this is a great club. The players go out on the town while the directors do the training'.

No trip could be complete without a story revolving around Tom McNiven. One evening Tom decided to make a visit to a primitive toilet in one of the poorer parts of town. While doing the 'business' he managed to drop his wallet down what was merely a hole in a wooden plank. Knowing Tom, we were all surprised that he didn't dive in head first after it, but after fishing around he eventually recovered the pouch covered in an unmentionable substance. Strangely, Tom didn't seem to find the incident as funny as we did.

Although Eddie Turnbull could be a demanding taskmaster, during these trips abroad he could also be great company and he often used to regale us with countless stories over a few pints. He could be a very humorous raconteur, very different from his often abrasive personality in the dressing room or training ground, and we would sit around enthralled as he entertained us with his experiences in the navy during the war or tales about his early days in football.

However, it was soon back to the serious business and we warmed up for what would prove to be a momentous season with a three game tour of Ireland. In the past 12 months we had grown as a team, and the cup final humiliation apart, the previous campaign had been fairly successful but we were all well aware that much more would be expected from us in the season ahead. By now I had fully recovered from my broken ankle but obviously still lacked match fitness after such a long layoff, and quite honestly I found the going in Ireland tough. I played in two of the games picking up a slight injury against Home Farm and was replaced by Willie Murray who scored his first goal for the club in our 2-0 victory.

The former Motherwell player Wilson Humphries who had been manager of St Mirren until just a few months before, accompanied us on our trip to Ireland and no sooner had we arrived back in Edinburgh than he was offered the role of first team trainer. Wilson was a really nice man, and the perfect foil to Eddie's abrasiveness. I'm not sure how good he was on the finer points of the game but we all liked him a lot. The boss would still take the majority of the training leaving Wilson to deal with us on a one to one basis, but he was a good lad and great for team spirit. He had a peculiar party piece. One day in the dressing room he surprised us all by climbing onto a bench still in his street clothes. Lying flat on his back, he lifted his knees to his chest, drew a cigarette lighter from his pocket and proceeded to light his flatulence, the sheet of flame shooting across the dressing room. The players needless to say were in stitches, and from that day on Wilson was often requested to repeat the feat.

By this time the green-and-white hooped collar had been replaced by the more distinctive all-white crewe neck, and the white socks of the previous season discarded in favour of the traditional green topped by a broad white band. To my mind it was one of the best Hibs strips ever and I always felt a million dollars when wearing it.

The new season kicked off with the sponsored Drybrough Cup competition, an experimental tournament contested by the four top scoring sides in each division the previous season and had been designed to encourage more goals. There were some who considered the Drybrough Cup to be a second rate tournament, usually fans of sides that had failed to qualify, but make no mistake all the players took it very seriously. To win it, both Celtic and Rangers would probably have to be overcome, never the easiest of tasks.

The games were played under experimental rules that decreed that a player could only be offside inside a line drawn the width of the pitch 18 yards from goal and it was humorous to see Arthur Duncan lurking right on the line closely marked by two defenders while play continued in the other half of the field. Sometimes Arthur would decide to take a wander along the line and back, again closely followed by his shadows. I missed the first game, a 4-0 victory against Queen of the South but was back in time for the convincing 3-0 victory over Rangers at Easter Road on the Wednesday. Again there was only one side in it. Rangers as usual tried to nullify our fast flowing football with their by now expected physical approach, but by this time we could look after ourselves and they were found wanting. The only mystery is how it took us so long to open the scoring when Stanton blasted a magnificent Edwards chip past McCloy in the Rangers goal just seconds before the break. Two second half goals by Alan Gordon confirmed a victory that was never in any doubt, and we now had a great chance to avenge the humiliation of the cup final defeat in May with a meeting against Celtic in the final at Hampden.

In the final, two goals, the first inside four minutes by Alan Gordon after the Celtic goalkeeper Williams had failed to hold the ball, and another by the centre forward midway through the half, gave us a deserved interval lead. An own goal by McNeill put us three up, and with only half an hour left to play seemingly on easy street. We were in total control until crowd trouble on the terracing spilled over onto the pitch, causing the game to be held up for several minutes. For some reason the delay seemed to upset our rhythm, and spurred on by a rampant Jimmy Johnstone Celtic managed to draw level and would possibly have won the game had it gone on any longer. In the interval before the extra 30 minutes the tactically astute Turnbull came into his own. As well as his inspiring team talk he replaced Johnny Hamilton with Jimmy O'Rourke. The move paid almost immediate dividends when Jimmy blasted a fantastic shot past Williams from 25 yards, Arthur Duncan wrapping it up in the dying seconds with a great strike from almost on the byline after cleverly deceiving Danny McGrain. In no way did the victory make up for the humiliating defeat in the Scottish Cup final, but it did go some small way to repair the damage, and was an almighty boost for our confidence.

Buoyed by the cup win we would lose only one of the League Cup section games, a 4-1 reverse to Aberdeen at Pittodrie. With Tony Higgins making his first team debut in place of Alan Gordon, the game was nothing like as one sided as the scoreline would suggest, three of Aberdeen's goals coming in a 13 minute spell in the first half. The main talking point came as we were beginning to claw ourselves back into the game. The Aberdeen centre forward Joe Harper was caught several yards offside after a quick break, the ball travelling back to Herriot who side footed it up field for the free kick to be taken as Harper retreated. Quick to realise that the referee had failed to blow for offside, Harper lobbed the ball over the stranded Herriot to end Hibs' interest in the match. Needless to say we were all furious, but the goal was allowed to stand, a lesson learned if needed that you should always play to the whistle

We defeated Aberdeen 2-1 in the return match in Edinburgh with goals from Duncan and O'Rourke but it was not enough to dislodge them from the top of the group table on goal average, although this was not too much of a problem as for the first time the top two sides would go forward into the qualifying stages. I learned later that the game against Aberdeen was the first ever outing of an 11 that would soon become known as Turnbull's Tornadoes:

HERRIOT, BROWNLIE AND SCHAEDLER; STANTON, BLACK AND BLACKLEY; EDWARDS, O'ROURKE, GORDON, CROPLEY AND DUNCAN. SUB: HAMILTON.

By this time we were all starting to sense that something special was about to happen. As well as being a highly organised and disciplined side that could play a bit, we all got on well together. There were no real cliques and this all went some way in creating a happy environment.

So far that season I had not managed to get on the score sheet myself. This was not proving to be a great problem as the goals were coming from all over the pitch, but I eventually opened my account in yet another 2-0 victory over Hearts at Easter Road, Pat Stanton notching the other. It had now been four years since Hearts had even scored against us and this game proved to be no different. Much to the surprise of the large crowd inside Easter Road we took the field wearing all green jerseys with white collars and cuffs, a strip presumably designed to counteract Hearts Ajax style jerseys that featured more white than normal. Taking complete control of the midfield right from the start our quick passing and movement had our opponents on the back foot throughout. Goalkeeper Garland had to be at his best, and although it took us until late in the game to make sure of the points, there was no question that the victory was deserved.

The win over our city rivals had boosted our confidence for the forthcoming midweek Cup Winners' Cup game against Sporting Lisbon in Portugal. The club had chartered a plane for the trip to Lisbon which I believe was the first time it had ever done so. To help offload the cost of the hire several dozen supporters travelled with the team, among them as guests of the club were the former Hibs players Tommy Preston and Gordon Smith who were both friends of Tom Hart.

We took the field in Lisbon to the unlikely strains of Hector Nicol's record *Glory Glory to the Hibees* that the Portuguese officials had somehow managed to get a hold of, which we all thought was a really nice touch. Wearing dark purple jerseys with white collars and cuffs, we started the game well and in front of a huge crowd the home side were shaken when I hit the post inside the opening minutes. During the early part of the game Sporting were 'chasing purple shadows' as one Scottish newspaper put it the following morning, possibly surprised as Hibs, as was Turnbull's usual style in Europe, went into all-out attack right from the start. In fairness, Sporting, who were then managed by the former West Bromwich Albion and England player Ronnie Allan, were a very good side with some really fine players such as the Argentinean centre forward Hector Yazalde, who would win the Golden Boot the following year, and Chico who came on as a substitute. The home side scored twice in the second half after a couple of defensive mistakes by Jim Herriot, the first when he was caught off his line, the other when he slipped coming out for an easy ball leaving the goal gaping. Late in the game Arthur Duncan and Jimmy O'Rourke were causing all kinds of bother in the home penalty area and Arthur scored what could well have been an important away goal after a great crossfield pass from John Brownlie. After the game Eddie Turnbull had a run in with the Hibs director Sir John Bruce who had unfairly criticised our performance. Understandably, Turnbull was furious and complained vociferously to the chairman regarding what he thought were totally unjustified comments. In the dressing room afterwards he gathered us together to tell us that as far as he was concerned, we had put up the best away display of any Hibs team in Europe.

There was also the now well-known incident in the dressing room after the game when Turnbull upset a tray of watches that were being carried into the room as gifts for the players, leaving the comical Johnny Hamilton to retort: 'Time flies, eh boss.' Johnny was a very funny guy who was always good for a laugh and it was he who gave me the nickname 'Sodjer' after discovering that I had been born in Aldershot.

A fortnight later in Edinburgh with us again wearing the all green strip, over 30,000 crammed inside Easter Road to see us blow Sporting Lisbon away in 45 minutes of second half magic when they just didn't have an answer. Alan Gordon had levelled the tie midway through the first half, only for the brilliant Yazalde to beat Herriot from close range to give the visitors the overall lead. We had scored five against Dundee United during the second half of the League Cup game the previous midweek, and we again scored five in a fantastic second period against Sporting to win 6-1, leaving the fans to wonder just what the manager said to us during the interval. Contrary to what most people might think there was rarely any shouting or reading of the riot act. The master tactician would simply say: 'get your cup of tea then sit down and I will tell you how to beat this lot', and invariably he would get it just right.

During the game right half Chico, who had played so well against us in Lisbon after coming on as a substitute, went over the top on John Blackley. It was a sore one, and John took down his sock to reveal six stud marks on his shin. As I passed, Blackley whispered to me: 'if you get a chance, do him', as though he was asking the right person. Not to be outdone, the next time I got near Chico I put on my hardest face as if to say, 'I'm going to do you', only to be put in my place when he ran past telling me in perfect English to 'F**k Off'. That was my gas put at a peep.

As a team we were now firing on all cylinders, and a couple of weeks later poor Airdrie were the next to feel our wrath in the first leg of the League Cup quarter final at Broomfield. Even with the return game in Edinburgh still to come Airdrie were blasted out of the competition after another spectacular second half performance. That evening the entire team were outstanding and sometimes I could only stand and marvel at the magnificent football that was taking place all around me. Arthur Duncan scored his second hat-trick in a Hibs shirt, but for me the real hero of the evening was the former Broomfield ball boy John Brownlie who hailed from Caldercruix just a few miles outside Airdrie. To my mind, at that time John was undoubtedly the best right back in Europe and he scored twice against his boyhood heroes with spectacular drives. Alan Gordon scored the other, the final 6-2 scoreline greatly flattering the home side, who might well have conceded double figures.

We had been drawn against FC Besa from Albania in the next round of the Cup Winners' Cup and a 3-1 victory at Firhill on the Saturday kept our championship challenge very much alive and set us up for the midweek first leg of the European tie at Easter Road. With 21 goals scored in our last four games, we were quite clearly giving the fans what they wanted and this was confirmed when a crowd of well over 20,000 turned out to watch us against the unknowns from Albania. In what turned out to be an easy 7-1 victory, yet another five goals were scored in the second half making even this early progress into the next round a mere formality.

Besa were a very poor side in every sense of the word. The Albanian's took the field wearing what had at one time been rich cherry red jerseys that were now faded in the wash. The numbers on the back were quite clearly painted on, and most of them were wearing boots that seemed to date from just after the war. I opened the scoring in the 12th minute from my favourite distance of just a few inches, after a brilliant Alan Gordon right foot drive had come crashing back off the bar, and another goal a few minutes later by Jimmy O'Rourke made it all too easy against a side who at their best were just honest triers. Another two from O'Rourke, two from Duncan and another by Brownlie, all scored inside a breath-taking 12 minute burst in the second half killed the tie stone dead, although the plucky Albanians managed to claw one back in one of their rare forays over the half way line. At the after match reception all the Besa players turned up wearing matching cheap anoraks and what looked like plastic sandals, and we couldn't quite believe it as they literally gorged themselves on the refreshments provided as if they had never seen good food in their lives. We would come to understand matters much better in Albania in a few weeks' time. We were told later that some Albanian players had even purchased TV's from a discount warehouse in the city, and I wondered just how they would have coped with the porn shops of Denmark in the previous round.

The result set us up nicely for the away leg in Albania, although strictly speaking nothing in the world could have prepared us for what lay in store during what would turn out to be a journey into hell.

Tom Hart had thought of everything. As well as taking our own food, the club had even hired the chef from the North British Hotel on Princes Street to accompany us on the trip. At Turnhouse we found that our flight to Tirana had been delayed and it was all downhill from there. We landed at a military airport just outside the capital Tiranha, the runway closely sandwiched between two huge mountains, and I can still remember looking out the window to see our plane surrounded by gun emplacements and MIG jet fighters. As we were boarding the ramshackle coach for the journey to our hotel a petrol tanker drew up alongside us and started to siphon the fuel from our aircraft just to make sure that it didn't try to take off again without permission. Things were already starting to look ominous. At what passed for an airport terminal there was a lively exchange when we were refused permission to load our own food onto the coach, and it was only after the heated intervention of chairman Tom Hart that the authorities eventually relented. For such a poor country on the way to our hotel I was amazed to see that the roads were extraordinarily wide, although they lacked street lights, the trees at the side of the road painted white, but apart from us there was literally no other traffic on them.

At the airport terminal, a dilapidated roofless building, we were met by an old man wearing a dishevelled army style uniform, carrying an ancient gun that looked as if it wouldn't have worked, although by his unwelcoming demeanour none of us would have been prepared to take the risk of finding out. While the food was being unloaded at the hotel an apple dropped to the ground. A watching youngster moved to pick it up, but quickly drew back to look first for acceptance from the watching commissar who nodded. The clearly frightened kid then proceeded to return the apple to its box. At the hotel we found our accommodation to be unbelievably basic. Neither the radios or primitive plumbing system was in working order, but fortunately director Jimmy Kerr had been a plumber and we took advantage of his expertise to effect temporary repairs. Although we had been allowed to offload our own food from the coach we were then refused the use of the kitchens, the players served with unpalatable meals that consisted mainly of what appeared to be horsemeat with chips resembling tasteless crisps. It was truly disgusting, most of us finding the concoction totally inedible and it was only after yet another lengthy confrontation that we were eventually allowed to cook our own food. We had also been informed in no uncertain terms that we were not allowed to leave the hotel without an official guide, a warning that was totally unnecessary, as in all reality there was nothing to see or anywhere interesting to visit. I found the poverty in the country to be truly heart-breaking, the sight of men, women and children walking around in clothes that were only one step removed from rags, made me appreciate my upbringing in a council house in Scotland all the more. The poorly stocked shops provided little in the way of choice, although several had what seemed to be communal television sets in the front shop, many surrounded by large groups of people.

It seemed as if every effort was being made to make our stay as unpleasant as possible and we were even refused transport to take us for a training session that afternoon, the authorities only relenting after yet another lengthy dispute. Just hours before kick-off we were told that the game had now been switched from Tirana to Durres 25 miles away, but by this time we'd had more than enough and just wanted to get the game over with and return home as soon as possible.

In what was no more than a nothing match after the first leg scoreline, our main objective was to avoid injury on a pitch that was worse than many of the public parks back home. With Herriot and McArthur both injured, goalkeeper Bobby Robertson again proved an able understudy against a side that were keen but poor, and in front of a full house of excitable Besa fans, an Alan Gordon goal in the second half was enough to give us what in the exceptionally trying circumstances was a credible 1-1 draw. In contrast to the rest of his 'teammates' one of the better Besa players was wearing a jersey in far better condition than the rest and also different coloured shorts and socks, so we guessed that he might be a 'ringer' brought in from another side. We had originally been told that it would not be possible to leave until morning, but immediately after the final whistle we were ordered to report to the airport at once for our flight home, a journey

CROPS: THE ALEX CROPLEY STORY

that could not come a second too soon for all of us. In the dressing room after the game Eddie Turnbull thanked us for putting up with what had been truly awful conditions since our arrival in the country, and I believe that Hibs later forwarded an official complaint to UEFA. Even then our nightmare was far from over. Instead of landing at Turnhouse as intended, our return flight had to be diverted to Glasgow, the final part of what had been a journey into hell completed by coach.

There was a humorous footnote to the affair. We arrived back at Easter Road with mountains of food that had remained unused because of the constant disputes in Albania. Rather than it go to waste several of the players were about to take some home. Tom McNiven immediately jumped in to tell them in no uncertain terms that the food was the property of Hibernian Football Club and was to be left alone. Outside the ground a short while later some of the players were in a car discussing the trip, when to their surprise they saw McNiven surreptitiously peek both ways outside the stadium door before emerging with a huge box of groceries.

As well as our good run in Europe, the victory over Airdrie had also presented us with a passage into the semi-finals of the League Cup and a game against who else but Rangers? The game at Hampden turned out to be a scrappy affair packed with stoppages against a physical, strong and hardworking team that employed their usual tight marking and hard tackling tactics. We were well below our best but still proved far too good for a Rangers side that had no one to match the trickery of Alex Edwards, the composure of John Blackley, or the directness of match winner John Brownlie. Level at the interval, a quite sensational second half solo goal by Brownlie was enough to win any game. Collecting a pass on the halfway line the full back proceeded to run 40 lung bursting yards through the middle of the Rangers defence, evading several lunging tackles on the way, before crashing an unstoppable shot past McCloy from just outside the box. John would later tell us that he was so exhausted after the run that he couldn't have gone any further, and just hit the ball more in hope than anticipation. We managed to hold out quite comfortably in the end except for a late scare when a Matheson shot whizzed just past the post in the final minute, but we had done more than enough to earn a passage into the cup final and yet another meeting with Celtic.

By now we were a highly disciplined, superbly organised, confident and fast moving side. Our team spirit and camaraderie was second to none, and as far as the players were concerned each game just couldn't come fast enough. Although we would be up against one of the best sides in Europe at that time, we made our way to Hampden for the League Cup final in buoyant mood. Since the start of the season we had improved out of all recognition, our confidence growing by the week, and we knew that it was not beyond us to return to Edinburgh with the cup. I remember it being a wet damp overcast afternoon as the teams took the field at Hampden, but we were heartened by the encouragement we received from the huge Hibs support among the near 72,000 crowd that had packed into the stadium. I was up against Pat McCluskey, a well-built player in the John Greig mould although not nearly as good as the Rangers captain, and I more than held my own against the rugged defender. A pretty unexciting first half ended goalless with very few near things at either end, except when Billy McNeill almost put the ball through his own net seconds before the half time whistle, and the Celtic goalkeeper Evan William's saving a quite magnificent Pat Stanton header from the resulting corner. After the interval it was a different story. We knew we had played well in the opening 45 minutes and we emerged from the tunnel in a confident mood to a rousing welcome from the Hibs fans who mainly occupied the covered end of the ground away to our left.

Midway through the half McNeill barged Alan Gordon from the ball 20 yards from goal to concede a free kick, disputed as always by the Celtic captain. With the Celtic defence expecting a direct shot, Edwards cheekily lifted the ball over the defensive wall to find Pat Stanton. At first I thought that Pat had missed his chance when he took an extra step to his right, but he hesitated only briefly before crashing a great shot into the roof of the net. Six minutes later we were two up after a quite magnificent cross by Stanton from the right wing allowed Jimmy O'Rourke to bullet a header past Williams from the edge of the six-yard box. We were now really on song and could well have scored more, particularly when Stanton hit the post with a wicked shot from outside the box. Alan Gordon later blasted the ball against McNeill from close range when it seemed easier to score, and although Dalglish pulled one back late in the game we held out comfortably until the final whistle. We had all played well, our passing and movement fantastic, but particular mention must be made of captain Pat Stanton. I sometimes thought that Pat didn't really know just how good a player he was. If he played well, Hibs played well. I once mentioned in an interview that perhaps he was not an ideal captain but what I meant was that he was not one to shout and roar encouragement. Pat did it by example, tirelessly and seemingly effortlessly, gliding from one end to another for the 90 minutes. Great in the air and a fantastic passer of the ball, he read the game well and his at times lazy style sometimes appeared to make it look all too simple. He was once described by the Scotland manager Tommy Docherty as a better player than Bobby Moore, and one can only speculate at the number of caps he would undoubtedly have won had he played his entire career with either of the two big Glasgow clubs. But more than that, as well as being a great player, Pat was, and is, a great lad; so unassuming and genuinely modest despite all that he has achieved in the game and it was a great privilege playing alongside him, both for Hibs and Scotland.

At the final whistle we all made our way to the end where most of our fans had congregated where we received a rousing reception from the ecstatic hordes who had just witnessed the first Hibs side in living memory to lift a cup. The Celtic manager Jock Stein being the great sportsman that he was, held back his obvious disappointment to congratulate each and every one of us as we left the field, a fantastic gesture.

After receiving the cup from Glasgow Lord Provost Sir William Gray we were met in the dressing room by an absolutely ecstatic Eddie Turnbull, Tom Hart and the rest of the directors and staff before making our way to Edinburgh a little later. At the Maybury Roadhouse we boarded the open topped bus, a vehicle that had so often been found to be surplus to requirements after cup finals involving Hibs, to make a quite emotional journey through the town to the North British Hotel on Princes Street for the post-match reception. Everywhere the streets were packed with thousands of well-wishers, not just football fans, but ordinary people who were all aware of just what the win meant for Edinburgh, the emotional journey through the streets of the capital made even more special for those of us who had been brought up in the city. It was a freezing cold night but the hair standing on the back of my neck had nothing to do with the temperature, and the journey through the town remains one of the highlights of my career. At the east end of Princes Street the crowds were so dense that the bus had great difficulty in making its way to the doors of the hotel. Once inside, the huge crowd that was blocking the surrounding streets refused to disperse, continually demanding that we show them the cup from the balcony. Both my parents were at the reception along with my brother Tam and a couple of friends and it was a highly emotional affair. As you can imagine it turned out to be a fantastic night but I was far too high to get drunk.

Hibs fanatic Eric Stevenson would later relate that he had been expected to play for Ayr United that afternoon but had decided to attend the cup final instead. Informed on the Monday morning by his manager, the former Hibs player Ally MacLeod, that he was being fined two weeks wages for missing the game, Eric considered it money well spent to see his boyhood heroes lift the cup.

By that time the press had dubbed us 'Turnbull's Tornadoes' but the side was more than just the 11 that were selected most weeks. During the season Johnny Hamilton and John Hazel each made several appearances, often from the subs bench, with the occasional outing for Bobby Robertson, Jim McArthur and Willie McEwan. John Hazel was a very good player, but to my mind he was far too easy going at times and perhaps lacked the desire of the rest of the side. He would move to Morton the following season, ending a career that had promised so much at Alloa after a spell with East Stirling. Hammy was the joker of the pack. Another really good player with a good football brain, he too probably lacked the necessary desire. I often felt that John's mind was elsewhere, probably in the direction of Glasgow. He was a rabid Rangers supporter and would soon realise his life's ambition with a move to Ibrox. At that time we had had a settled side except for injury and it must have been incredibly difficult for both players to fit into a team that knew each other's style of play so well. Goalkeeper Bobby Robertson had proved a reliable stand-in for Jim Herriot, featuring from the start not only in Europe but in a couple of the League Cup games, and was often a substitute. Bobby had performed well when required but struggled to make the first team jersey his own particularly after the signing of Jim McArthur from Cowdenbeath during the season. After a bright start at the club Willie McEwan seemed to lose his way. I don't think the manager really fancied Willie, and he too would soon be on his way, in his case to a long career both as a player and manager in England.

The cup win was just the start of an incredible few weeks for the club. The following Saturday at Easter Road both the Drybrough and League Cups were paraded in front of the fans before the game against Ayr United on a motorised grass cutter. Maybe the club could have organised the celebrations a bit better, but the ecstatic hordes on the terracing didn't seem to care. Ayr were unfortunate to be meeting us at that particular moment and they were quite literally blown away as we turned on what was perhaps our best performance of the season.

I opened the scoring after just 11 seconds, both Jimmy O'Rourke and Alan Gordon notching a hat-trick as we beat the Somerset Park side 8-1. Perhaps fittingly, captain Pat Stanton scored the other. It was real exhibition stuff as we proceeded to tear poor Ayr apart and no side in the country would have lived with us that afternoon. Alan Gordon's third goal was Hibs' 100th of the season and we had not even reached the halfway point yet. In a vintage five star performance, no Hibs player was better than the other, everyone from goalkeeper Jim Herriot to Arthur Duncan on the left wing playing their part, even substitute Kenny Davidson getting in on the act.

A hard fought 1-1 draw at Parkhead against a wounded Celtic side who were absolutely desperate for revenge after the defeat at Hampden, was followed by a 3-2 victory against Aberdeen at Easter Road, then it was on to Tynecastle for the New Years Day derby.

January 1 1973 was a historic day in more ways than one. It was Britain's first day as a member of the European Economic Community, or the Common Market as it later became better known. At that time both the Edinburgh clubs were going well. We were scoring goals for fun while Hearts were conceding very few, and it promised to be an interesting contest.

It was also the 100th league meeting between the sides since automatic promotion had been introduced just after the First World War, with the Gorgie side one ahead in the series. We trained as usual on the morning of the game, nothing too strenuous, just light exercises. The boss was a great one for making things interesting and varied, and that morning we practised penalties, but with a difference. This time the kicker had to tell the goalkeeper just where he was going to place the ball and still try to beat him. There's always one, however, and Hammy being Hammy pointed to one side and shot into the other leaving Turnbull shaking his head, but it was all good fun and great for team spirit.

Strangely, I was not overly nervous before the start. As a team we treated every match the same, taking it one game at a time and refusing to look too far ahead. Before we left the dressing room Turnbull simply dotted the I's and crossed the T's as he used to describe it. It was just a simple, 'play your own game lads', telling Jim Black to win the headers, and instructing Erich to win the ball then give it to someone who could use it. Never did we concentrate on the strengths or weaknesses of the other side, only on our own game.

There was a good crowd inside the stadium as the teams took

the field with hundreds more outside still trying to gain admittance. Many latecomers would miss several of the goals, while hundreds already inside the ground would leave early. Hearts missed a couple of great chances to take the lead in the opening minutes, none better than an effort by Donald Park who scuffed the ball wide from inside the penalty area with the goal gaping. How a goal then might have changed things! As against Ayr United a few weeks before, we soon got into the groove and from then on we were literally unplayable. We were overloaded with football, a team full of talent, and a Hearts side that had conceded only three goals in the previous 13 hours of football, had already conceded three in the opening 26 minutes. Jimmy O'Rourke started the rout when he ghosted into the Hearts box to blast past Garland from a throw in, Alan Gordon adding a second a few minutes later when he cleverly chested down an Alex Edwards cross to fire home almost in the one movement. Arthur Duncan scored a third with a great solo run. Although they were three behind the Hearts fans were still in good voice but they were silenced a few minutes later when I scored with a left foot volley from well outside the box. The Hearts defender Eddie Thomson could only manage to clear an effort from Arthur Duncan high into the air. I remember the ball seeming to take an age in coming down and I was slightly flat footed as I crashed an unstoppable shot past the Hearts goalkeeper. There was still almost an hour to play but the game was already as good as over. Duncan scored his own second and our fifth with a fortuitous header that just managed to evade the grasping fingers of Garland, Jimmy O'Rourke coming agonisingly close to making it six with a cute flick over Hearts defensive wall at a free kick. The move was reminiscent of Hibs' first goal against Celtic in the League Cup final, and the audacious effort was fully deserving of a goal.

A few minutes before the break I was involved in an incident with the Hearts captain Alan Anderson who had either fouled me or tried to kick me. Although it was not my style, the occasion had possibly got the better of me and I told him to 'F**k Off', also politely enquiring as to the score. I thought Alan was going to explode. A short while later the half time whistle found me not far from the tunnel. Looking up I could see Anderson a fair distance away start to walk quickly in my direction before starting to break into a run. I continued to walk nonchalantly towards the tunnel, somehow attempting to walk nonchalantly faster and faster before the centre half, who believe me is a big man, could catch up with me. We came together just as I was about to enter the dressing room, only for Eddie Turnbull to come between us with the very welcoming words: 'On your way big man'.

Hearts restarted the second half with a brief flurry and within minutes centre forward Donald Ford had the ball in the net only for it to be ruled offside. It was Donald's 300th game in a Hearts jersey and he had yet to score against Hibs. Further goals by Jim O'Rourke and a header by Alan Gordon with 15 minutes remaining killed a game that had been all but dead since midway through the first half. Understandably in the dressing room after the final whistle we were all euphoric, none more so than Eddie Turnbull, who still had the difficult task of offering his commiserations to the Hearts manager Bobby Seith, who was a good friend. Most of the other players particularly Pat Stanton, Jimmy O'Rourke and Alan Gordon were all aware that it was a historic victory, one that saw us sitting at the top of the table, but honestly, to me it was just another, albeit particularly satisfying, win.

Alan Anderson and I made up after the game, the Hearts captain telling me that he wouldn't have done anything rash, but I was still pleased that the boss's intervention had prevented me from finding out.

After the game I went home to my granny's house in Northfield for dinner with the family. As usual my dad didn't have much to say about the game, but my mum, who came from a Hibs family was absolutely delighted, and we all watched the highlights on TV. Later, Pat, Jimmy, Alan and I all went out for a few very satisfying drinks. The next day the papers were understandably highly complementary regarding our performance. One described us as 'not only the team of the moment, but also the team of the future'. Another: 'Invincible Hibs now look outstanding odds on favourites to add to the two trophies already won'. Yet another:

> There were no weaknesses in this side. Every Hibs player played his part, but Alex Cropley in midfield was outstanding, and on this display Alan Gordon is surely the best centre forward in Scotland.

But perhaps the *Daily Record* summed it up best: 'with magic touches reminiscent of Real Madrid, Hibs have a team to take on the world'.

There was one slight downside. At that time I was engaged to Liz Malcolm who would later become my wife. Liz's brother Jim, however, was a massive Hearts fan and for several weeks after the game, he refused to even speak to me. I had met Liz in a city centre pub some time before and had been attracted to her right from the start. Being my shy self it took me several months before I could even say hello, but after the ice was broken we eventually got together.

We were all still buzzing after our victory at Tynecastle when we faced East Fife in a league match at Easter Road on the Saturday, a game that would turn out to have disastrous consequences for the club. Perhaps it was an anti-climax after such a great result at Tynecastle, but we really struggled against dogged and hard to break down opponents. With all due respect to East Fife, we came crashing down to their level, and I personally had a very poor game. Just before half time, John Brownlie, who was then playing the best football of his career, was involved in an accidental clash with left back Printy near the tunnel, leaving him with a leg broken in two places. John had a habit of stretching to drag the ball back, sometimes stretching too far and this might well have contributed to the unfortunate accident. John's injury was a colossal blow not only for Hibs, but also for the watching Willie Ormond who had just replaced Tommy Docherty as the Scotland manager, and he would now miss the services of perhaps the most influential full back in the country for many months. Alex Edwards had been the victim of cynical foul challenges by both Walter Borthwick and John Love all afternoon, each appearing to take turns in fouling the volatile Fifer. Perhaps understandably, Alex finally snapped and he threw the ball at Love after a disputed throw-in. In what appeared to be a continuation of a long running feud between the pair, the Hibs player was booked for his part in the incident.

East Fife had tried everything to negate our fast flowing game and almost succeeded until Alan Gordon scored the only goal of the game late on, a goal incidentally that kept us on top of the table. Packing their goalmouth tightly and prepared to concede countless fouls, it was clear that Pat Quinn's team had come to settle for a point and they were booed off at the end. In the dressing room after the game the mood was solemn, all of us aware that not only had we lost the services of a key player, but that we had potentially lost the services of another after the suspension of Edwards that was certain to follow. I visited John in the Royal Infirmary later that evening to find him obviously in a subdued mood. Having been there myself a couple of times in recent years I understood more than most just what he was going through at that particular time.

Alex Edwards booking would later prove expensive for the club, taking him over the limit, and he would soon receive what many considered to be an unjust and somewhat savage eight week suspension. It was probably difficult to defend 'Mickey's' disciplinary record, having appeared before the committee several times before, but others with an equally bad record had often received a much less severe sentence, and I wondered if he was being made an example of. I also thought that the situation left the diminutive midfield player slightly disillusioned with the game, and I'm not sure if he was ever quite the same player afterwards.

John Brownlie's horrific injury had given Des Bremner a quicker than expected promotion and he made his first team debut the following Saturday in an away defeat to Dundee United, a result that was a severe blow to our championship aspirations. Bremner had been signed from Highland League side Deveronvale only a few months before and at that time I didn't think that he was much of a player, although admittedly he had a hard act to follow in John Brownlie and I had a great deal of sympathy for him. To give Des his due it must have been extremely difficult for such an inexperienced youngster to come into such a well organised and disciplined side who all knew each other's strengths and weaknesses. Obviously Des didn't know the system and our flow down the right-hand side stuttered. Before, everything had come from either Brownlie or John Blackley who started the attacks from the back. Des would soon improve and in time would become an influential figure at Easter Road in his own right before a move to Aston Villa, and a European Cup winners medal.

These were exciting times at the club. In mid-January we were invited to a Civic Reception at the City Chambers, where Lord Provost Jack Kane paid tribute to the honour and prestige that we had brought to the city, adding,

> There have been great teams at Easter Road before, but the present side outshines even the Famous Five. The players are a tribute to their manager, and are destined to get even better.

It was also around this time that we became pop stars. Directed by then well-known composer and Hibs fan Johnny Keating, who had written the popular theme tune for the television series *Z-Cars*. We recorded an 8-inch single entitled 'Hibernian give us a goal' in prefabricated huts in the playground of Holy Cross School in Trinity. The words for the flip side: 'Turnbull's Tornadoes', had been written by chairman Tom Hart's wife Sheila, and the record was first aired at the club's annual dinner at the North British Hotel a few days before the Civic Reception. Using a background of pre-recorded music and no rehearsal to speak of, the entire session was over in no time at all, and we were pleasantly surprised at the quality of the finished product. It wasn't exactly Top of the Pops material, but apparently some of the management team at EMI were of the opinion that it was one of the best football records they had ever heard, and it sold well in the music stores throughout the area.

A 2-0 victory over Morton in the Scottish Cup had paired us yet again against Rangers in the next round, the fifth year in succession that we had faced each other in the Scottish Cup. Although it again required a replay to separate the teams, this time the Ibrox men came out on top in a punishing game. Once again Rangers had been unable to match us in skill, and had adopted their usual rugged spoiling approach. Prepared to concede countless fouls to disrupt our flow, this time their tactics proved successful, and they scored the winner from the penalty spot near the end. After the humiliation at the hands of Celtic in the final the previous May we had been determined to make up for the heavy defeat, both for ourselves and for the fans, and we were bitterly disappointed at what had been our first defeat in the Scottish Cup at Easter Road for 11 years.

Just before the cup ties I had again been called into the Under 23's side to face England at Rugby Park. In those days the Under 23's games were capable of attracting big crowds, including scouts from many of the top teams, the players only too aware that they were in the shop window. I remember England as a big physical side, and included in their line-up was Dennis Mortimer, then with Coventry City, who I would later play alongside at Aston Villa. Although we lost 2-1, we were not a bad side ourselves with players like John McGovern then with Derby County, Rab Prentice of Hearts, and my roommate Asa Hartford of West Bromwich Albion, who's recent much publicised move to Leeds United had been called off after it was discovered he had a hole in the heart.

Some indifferent results saw Hibs drop to third place in the table. Although we were still well in contention, it now seemed as though Europe was our best chance of picking up more silverware. For the game against the Yugoslavian side Hajduk Split in the third round of the Cup Winners' Cup at Easter Road, Eddie Turnbull sprang a surprise by including the untried John Salton in the squad. But a bigger surprise by far, and one that also caught the players completely unawares,

CROPS: THE ALEX CROPLEY STORY

was the inclusion of Alex Edwards, who although suspended from domestic competition was eligible to play in Europe.

We knew very little about our opponents, but Hajduk Split turned out to be a decent side who created several chances, although I felt that we should really have won by more than the 4-2 scoreline. Again wearing the all green jerseys, we adopted our usual European tactics of going for our opponents straight from the first whistle, but found Hajduk difficult to subdue, and they matched us man for man even after Alan Gordon had given us the lead after only six minutes from an Edwards cross. Although the visitors continued to look dangerous on the break, another goal by Gordon after 25 minutes brought the huge partisan crowd numbering just under 30,000 to life. Just when they looked like being completely overrun, Hajduk scored what could well have turned out to be an important away goal. The loss of the goal now made it imperative that we score again and a strike by Arthur Duncan midway through the second half and another by Alan Gordon, his hat-trick, appeared to put us on easy street. We survived a couple of scary moments late in the game, particularly when a Jerkovic shot hit the post only for the ball to rebound into the arms of Herriot, but as the fans were beginning to make their way to the exits, we lost another vital away goal after a complete shambles in our penalty area, after Bremner had failed to clear a corner from the right, allowing outside right Hlevnjac to score. I myself had a particularly poor game, failing completely to get to grips with right half Buijan and I was replaced by Jimmy O'Rourke in the second half. An air of despondency hung over the stadium at the final whistle and we were all aware that we had let ourselves down. Although we were still confident of progressing into the next round, in the space of a few minutes we had surrendered what appeared to be an almost unassailable lead, and knew that the Yugoslavs would now probably be the bookies favourites to progress into the semi-finals. Alan Gordon's hat-trick had been his 41st goal of the season in all competitions, and his third treble for the club including the four he had scored against Airdrie a few weeks earlier. It was also the tenth hat-trick by a Hibs player that season, O'Rourke with six and Duncan one.

In the return game in Split we performed far better than the 3-0 scoreline would suggest but managed to surrender our first leg lead quite comfortably courtesy of some shocking defending. The loss of two goals in under six minutes when Herriot, who had a really bad night, missed easy crosses that both led to goals, put us behind on the away goals ruling. The midfield trio of myself, Pat Stanton and Alex Edwards failed completely to get to grips with the game, hesitant and second to every ball, and only Jim Black could be exempt from criticism, the centre half performing well in spite of the disastrous defending that was going on all around him. As in the first game at Easter Road we found our opponents to be a decent side, sharp and with great movement, but on a tight pitch and surrounded by a huge hostile crowd we failed to do ourselves justice and it was no surprise when they scored a third a few minutes into the second half after Herriot had again failed to collect a simple cross, the inrushing Blackley turning the ball into his own net in attempting to clear. I had a dreadful game and was again replaced midway through the half, this time by Bobby Smith who was making his European debut. Things were to get even worse. Five minutes from time Erich Schaedler dislocated his right shoulder after a heavy tackle, and was replaced by Jimmy O'Rourke. The rugged full back, one of the mainstays in our defence, was now expected to miss the rest of the season.

As you can imagine the post-match reception was a very flat affair. Eddie Turnbull would relate in later years that he had been confident of going all the way to the final in Solonika, possibly even winning the competition, and that the defeat in Split had caused him to contemplate his future in the game. The disastrous evening in Yugoslavia had completely knocked the heart from him and things would never quite be the same again. I have been told since that many Hibs fans had also been so confident of us at least reaching the final that they were already making provisional arrangements to travel to the game.

If Eddie Turnbull had been contemplating his future, then so was I. Although I was happy at Hibs, there were constant stories in the press linking me with other clubs, mainly from England, and I was beginning to wonder if it was time for a change. It was no big deal, and I was in no hurry to go, but looking back the seeds had already been planted in my mind.

Amazingly Erich Schaedler's dislocated shoulder would mean him missing only one game, a dreadful 0-0 draw against Arbroath, and he was replaced by Willie McEwan who was making one of his rare appearances in the first team. There had also been debuts for Tom Stevens in a 1-0 defeat by Motherwell, and Derek Spalding in a 1-1 draw with Ayr United. There had also been the occasional game for Tony Higgins. Spalding looked useful, but in truth I didn't think that Tony Higgins was much of a player. He was exceptionally good on the ball for such a big man and had a good football brain, but he could also be quite cumbersome, and to my mind he was far too slow to fit into such a fast, smooth-moving side. However, Tony would go on to do quite well for himself in the game scoring over 30 goals from well over a hundred appearances for Hibs before a move to Partick Thistle. He would later be elected chairman of the Scottish Professional Players Union, and is now the highly respected Scottish representative of FIFPro, the international footballers' union.

The final few weeks of the season were a huge anti-climax after the earlier expectation and we could only manage two draws from our final six games. In many ways it had been an incredible journey, but even with Alex Edwards back for the last few weeks, in the end it was far too little too late. To lose the services of two such influential players as Brownlie and Edwards for a large part of the season and still be expected to compete proved beyond even the capabilities of a talented side like Hibs, and we could only manage to finish in third place in the table.

In the final game of the season at Easter Road the Hibs fans were left to contemplate just what might have been as Celtic won their eighth championship in a row with a somewhat flattering 3-0 victory.

During the season Alan Gordon had scored 42 goals in all games, Jimmy O'Rourke 34 and Arthur Duncan 23, a total of just one less than 100 between the three which was a quite incredible feat. With the exception of the goalkeepers and Jim Black all the other regular first team players including both full backs had managed to get on the score sheet. In comparison by the end of the season I had weighed in with what for me was a measly ten in all games, which was quite a few less than I would have been happy with.

At the end of what had otherwise been a fantastically successful season Willie McEwan, Bertie Auld, Johnny Hamilton and Jim Herriot were all given free transfers. I was surprised that Hammy had been freed given that he had been the man in possession at the end of the season, but he would soon sign for his beloved Rangers. Bertie joined the backroom staff at Easter Road but there was probably no surprise, especially after the earlier signing of Jim McArthur, that Herriot had been released, poor Jim perhaps paying heavily for his dreadful performance against Hajduk Split in Yugoslavia.

Mum at North Berwick around 1942.

Dad while playing for Aldershot Town around the time of my birth.

The Edinburgh Schools side before the game against Glasgow at Tynecastle in 1966. I am on the extreme right of the front row. Kenny Watson, later to sign for Rangers, is second from left in the same row. On his right is Rab Kerr who had trials with Leicester City and on his left is Mike Reilly, now chairman of the Hibs Supporters' Club. Immediately behind me is George Wood who would sign for Hearts. Standing next to George is Kenny Chisholm who would accompany me to Burnley for trials.

One of my first individual photos at Hibs, taken around the late 1960s. You can see why all the girls fell for me!

Another early shot of me at Easter Road, taken around 1972.

The Hibs reserve side around 1968–69.
Back row, left to right: Murphy, Simpson, Davis, Baines, Wilkinson, Madsen, Devlin.
Front: O'Rourke, McEwan, Hunter, McPaul, Cropley.

The future Hibs manager Willie MacFarlane presenting a cup to the well-known Edinburgh juvenile side Melbourne Thistle. Receiving the cup is captain Alan Munro who would later become a director at Easter Road. My brother Tam is at the extreme right of the back row and my soon-to-be colleague at Hibs, Erich Schaedler, is middle of the front row. Dennis Nelson who would also sign for Hibs is on Erich's left.

Manager Willie MacFarlane who took over from Shankly and had enough faith in me to encourage me to turn full-time.

My dad and I with my English birth certificate after I had been selected for Scotland's game against Portugal in 1971.

The Hibs squad when Eddie Turnbull first became manager of Hibs in 1971.
Back row, left to right: Duncan, Shevlane, Black, Pryce, Baines, Gillett, Brownlie, Baker, Fraser (coach).
Middle: McNiven (physio), Mathieson, O'Rourke, Stanton, Grant, Gordon, Blackley, Miller, Hazel, Nelson.
Front: Davidson, Pringle, Graham, Hamilton, McEwan, Schaedler, Cropley, Auld, Young, Stevenson.

The Scotland squad at Largs before the game against Portugal.
Back row, left to right: Tommy Docherty (manager), Hay (Celtic), Colquhoun (Sheffield United),
Wilson (Arsenal), Stanton (Hibs), Graham (Arsenal), Jardine (Rangers), McNiven (Hibs physio).
Front: Johnstone (Celtic), Gemmill (Derby County), Bremner (Leeds United), Cropley (Hibs)
O'Hare (Derby County).

Turning Rodriques of Portugal inside out before hitting the post with my shot.

The Hibs captain Pat Stanton lifting the League Cup after our victory against Celtic in the 1972 final at Hampden.

In the Hampden dressing room with the League Cup. The happy Hibs players are from left to right: Black, O'Rourke, Brownlie, Hamilton, Cropley, Duncan, Stanton, Herriot.

The victorious Hibs players at the after-match celebrations at the North British Hotel on Princes Street.
Back row, left to right: Humphries, Cropley, McNiven, Edwards, Black, Gordon, Stanton and Schaedler.
Middle: Blackley, Hazel, Duncan, Brownlie, Hamilton and Herriot.
Front: Turnbull and O'Rourke.

Turnbull's Tornadoes with the both the League and Drybrough cups.
Back row left to right: Smith, Spalding, McArthur, Bremner, O'Rourke.
Middle: Turnbull (manager), Humphries (coach), Blackley, McGregor, Higgins, Brownlie, Black,
coaches Fraser and Auld.
Front: Edwards, Schaedler, Munro, Stanton, Gordon, Cropley, Duncan, McNiven (physio).

Jimmy O'Rourke scoring Hibs' sixth goal in the famous 7-0 victory over Hearts at Tynecastle.

Action from an East of Scotland game against Hearts at Easter Road. You can see by the packed terraces that games were then capable of attracting big crowds.
Left, Hazel, centre Oliver and Sneddon (both Hearts), right Cropley.

Alan Gordon scoring the winning goal against Celtic in the 1973 Drybrough Cup final. I am on the extreme left, puffing away like an old train.

Scoring our first goal from my favourite distance of a few inches in Hibs' 7-1 win against FC Besa after Alan Gordon's drive had come crashing back off the bar.

The celebrations after my first goal for Arsenal against Carlisle at Highbury.
I am being congratulated by John Radford who later told me I had the heart of a lion. The other Arsenal
players are McNab, Kidd and Kelly.

Slipping the ball past Manchester City's Corrigan in Arsenal's narrow 3-2 defeat at Highbury. The other
players are Pardoe (Manchester City), Ball (Arsenal) and Power (Manchester City).

Evading the despairing dive of Bryan King to open the scoring in Arsenal's 5-0 victory against Coventry City at Highbury.

Scoring Arsenal's third goal in the same game.

The Arsenal ⟨crest⟩ Football Club
Season 1975-1976

The Arsenal first team squad season 1975–76.
Back row left to right: Campbell (coach), Hornsby, Mancini, Matthews, Rimmer, Kidd, Barnett, Ross, Powling, Rostron Street (physio).
Front: Rice, Cropley, Nelson, Kelly, Radford, Mee (manager), Ball, Storey, Simpson, Armstrong, Brady.

Scoring Arsenal's second goal against Middlesbrough at Highbury. The others in the picture are goalkeeper Platt (Middlesbrough) and Kidd and Brady of Arsenal.

Scoring Arsenal's first goal in the League Cup tie against Everton at Highbury, September 1975.

Aston Villa versus Arsenal at Villa Park September 1975. I just fail to get on the end of a cross in our 2-0 defeat, watched by Villa's Edinburgh born Charlie Aitken and Arsenal's Brian Kidd. Eddie Kelly is an interested bystander in the background.

Arriving at Villa Park shortly after being collected from New Street station by the Villa chief scout Tony Barton.

Outside Villa Park that same evening.

Watching Villa play Norwich from the dugout. This was the game that convinced me that my immediate future lay in Birmingham.

Hidden behind the Sunderland defender just seconds before chipping goalkeeper Barry Siddall to score what was later acclaimed as a 'wonder goal'.

Siddall and his teammates can only look on as I am congratulated by Andy Gray.

The sports forum at the supporters' club on the evening I was to meet my long term partner, Pat. From left: local sports reporter Dave Leggett, the MC, myself and Gordon Smith.

The full Aston Villa playing Squad season 1977–78.
Back row, left to right: Stevenson, Young, Findlay, Burridge, Parsons, Spink, Evans, Linton.
Middle: Barton, Shorthouse, Evans, Buttress, Gregory, Gray, Smith, Hughes, Cowans, O'Dowd, Leonard, Richardson.
Second front: MacLaren, Deehan, Cropley, Phillips, Gidman, Saunders, Robson, Little, Mortimer, Carrodus, Downes.
Front: Jenkins, Gibson, Ollis, Ward, Beech, Hendry, Williams, Capaldi, Ormsby.

Meeting the Princess Royal and her husband, Mark Phillips, before the 1976 League Cup final against Everton at Wembley. From left: Mark, Phillips, Nicholl, Gray, Deehan, Phillips, myself, Robson, Burridge, Carrodus. Everton's Bob Latchford, who would miss the game, is on the extreme right of the photo.

A great action shot as Manchester United's Steve Coppell attempts to block my shot from hitting the post.

CHAPTER SEVEN

Enter Joe Harper
and a Penalty Disappointment in Europe

THE CUP WINS of the previous year had created greater expectation for the coming season. As was his way, Eddie Turnbull had little to say to us regarding any personal ambitions he may have had in an effort to deflect even more pressure from his players, but after the recent events he too would undoubtedly have had his own aspirations for the coming campaign. I myself was not too sure what the coming season would hold in store. I still felt we lacked the consistency of a truly great side destined for more honours. We had also lost three of the regular side that had performed so well during the first half of the previous season, players who would be difficult to adequately replace.

Kenny Davidson was now fully fit again after his broken leg, which was a huge bonus for us, but there was no such luck for John Brownlie who had needed yet another operation on his right leg during the summer. As usual the pre-season training under Turnbull was very exhausting for the first couple of weeks before we even saw a ball, but in the end we could have the satisfaction of perhaps being the fittest team in the country.

There were no wins in a three game pre-season trip to Denmark, Sweden and Norway, against what turned out to be very good sides. Naturally we had wanted to win the games, but we were aware that the short tour had only been arranged to sharpen our fitness before the trials that lay ahead, and there was no great concern on our part at departing without a victory.

As Drybrough Cup holders we were determined to retain our hold on the trophy and we faced St Mirren in the first round at Easter Road.

Ian Munro had been signed from the Paisley club during the summer along with Alex McGregor from Ayr United, and by a strange twist of fate Munro was making his debut against his former side. By this time Jim McArthur had replaced Jim Herriot who had made the journey in the opposite direction to Munro during the summer. McArthur was a very capable goalkeeper. Although a bit on the small side and not a great kicker of the ball, he was a great shot stopper and was every bit as good as Herriot in organising things at the back. Jim had made several first team appearances the previous season and we all had great confidence in him. He would prove to be another very good signing and would go on to give Hibs many years' service, eventually earning himself a testimonial.

Ian Munro became an instant hero to the Easter Road fans when he opened the scoring a few minutes into the second half against his former side. It was his first goal for Hibs, and although we were well below par as the Saints made us work hard for our 2-1 victory, it was enough to give us a passage into the semi-finals and another game against Rangers. The Ibrox side had been on a fantastic run of 27 games without defeat but that all came to an end at Easter Road after yet another titanic midweek two hour battle. Rangers as usual concentrated on their power play but by now we were well capable of handling ourselves in those situations. During the torrid 120 minutes, there was violence both on and off the park, with the police forced to enter the terracing several times to deal with trouble among the rival supporters. The violence on the field, however, had started much earlier, caused partly in my opinion by referee Webster who was far too lenient from the start, allowing numerous overzealous tackles to go unpunished. In the end, goals from Tony Higgins and Des Bremner, his first for the club, meant victory for the side that had concentrated on playing football, and we were through to yet another meeting with our by then regular nemesis in the final: Celtic.

After yet another gruelling 120 minutes in the final at Hampden, penalties were looming until Alan Gordon scored the only goal of the game in the very last minute to give us successive Drybrough Cup wins. We had now beaten Celtic in three consecutive cup finals since the humiliating defeat in the Scottish Cup just under 24 months before. Both sides had missed chances in a punishing opening 90 minutes. Celtic had been the stronger in the opening period but we finished the game much the better side. A strong wind had made conditions difficult for both sides as they each strove to make the important breakthrough. I started the game on the substitutes bench but came on to make a telling contribution. With only seconds of extra time remaining and both managers making arrangements for penalty kicks, I received a pass from Tony Higgins. My through ball was brilliantly collected on the run by Alan Gordon who found himself in the clear and he wasted no time in crashing the winning goal past the advancing Williams. The blustery conditions had made it an extremely tiring occasion for the players of both sides and, although I had spent the majority of the game on the bench, a photograph of the goal shows me appearing to be blowing out of my backside.

In the League Cup, once again we breezed through the section games winning five of the six against Morton, Ayr United and Dumbarton. In a satisfying 2-0 victory over Morton at Easter Road I scored both goals. The then Morton and former Hibs coach Jimmy Stevenson, who had been such a great help to me in the early days at Easter Road, whispered 'well done son', as I left the field, his words greatly appreciated. Jimmy had great faith in me as a youngster, and although I had just scored the goals that had defeated his side, I would like to think that in some small way I had repaid his confidence in me.

Pat Stanton made his 500th appearance for Hibs in the home victory against Dumbarton, but it was the return game at the aptly named Boghead that was to cause us so much bother. Jim McArthur had broken his thumb the previous Saturday, an injury that was expected to keep him sidelined for several weeks, and with only limited cover in the goalkeeping department, Turnbull wasted no time in signing the highly rated Irish international goalkeeper Roddy McKenzie from Airdrie for a fee reported to be around £8,000. Roddy, who was currently suspended by his club after a dispute involving a benefit payment was signed only on the morning of the Dumbarton game. We all rated McKenzie who was an extremely capable, athletic and acrobatic goalkeeper, but for some reason his time at Easter Road didn't go well. On his debut against Dumbarton, Roddy had what can only be described as a nightmare game, and he was clearly at fault for several of the goals, one when he rolled the ball too far in front of him, allowing Tom McAdam to nip in and score. To be fair to the goalkeeper, he had not played for a while, and in front of a poor crowd, at a poor stadium and on a poor pitch, none of us played to our capabilities as we conspired to lose 4-1.

Things were about to get even worse.

A couple of weeks after the debacle at Boghead and just eight months since our historic New Years Day victory at Tynecastle, this time we were soundly beaten by our city rivals Hearts, the game again played at the Gorgie ground. With significant personnel changes at both teams, Hearts were champing at the bit for revenge and came out of the traps much quicker than us, although it took a spectacular headed own goal by Schaedler to give them an interval lead. In the second half, three goals were scored in an unbelievable two minute burst. After Aird had made it 2-0, I scored to give us a chance when I clipped a 50-50 high ball from goalkeeper Garland's hands, a goal that probably would not be allowed nowadays. Only seconds later Donald Ford scored his first ever goal against Hibs to make it 3-1 and we never really recovered, the final 4-1 scoreline allowing Alan Anderson to enquire without even a hint of a smile as we left the field at the end: 'What's the f*****g score now?' Alan was a daunting opponent. Although he had the physique of an Adonis he was a bit on the slow side, but was a good tackler who never left you alone for a second and despite our earlier little altercation I had a lot of time for the player.

None of the goals conceded at Tynecastle had been McKenzie's fault, but Jim McArthur was soon back between the posts, and during his almost two years at Easter Road, Roddy would figure in only seven league games before a move to Clydebank at the start of the 1975–76 season.

Since the signing of Ian Munro, fans favourite Jimmy O'Rourke had also been finding it difficult to secure a regular start, often having to content himself with a place on the bench. I don't know if the boss ever really fancied Jimmy who was not the best tactically, but he was a great team player, and on song, a fantastic goal scorer who combined well up front with Alan Gordon, making and scoring many spectacular goals. It wasn't just Jimmy who was sometimes finding it difficult to secure a starting place, and for the opening few weeks of the new season the two of us often found ourselves sharing the bench. As already mentioned Ian Munro had been signed from St Mirren a few weeks before, possibly as a potential replacement for me, along with Alex McGregor from Ayr United. One morning as we were lining up to take part in a training exercise we watched both Munro and McGregor play in a small sided game. The astute Pat Stanton whispered to me that Munro was the player most likely to succeed because of his whole hearted attitude. Pat as usual would be proved right. 'Minnie' would make seven appearances for Scotland in-between moves to Rangers, St Mirren, Stoke City, Sunderland and Dundee, before returning to Easter Road in 1984, while sadly Alex failed to make a single appearance for the first team. McGregor was a nice big easy going guy, but found it difficult to break into such a talented side. He had great skill and pace but lacked a bit of heart and could easily be put off his game. He would later move to Shrewsbury, with a loan spell at West Ham, before ending his career with both my dad's old sides Aldershot and Farnborough Town.

We were drawn against the Icelandic side Keflavik in the UEFA Cup, the European games always greatly anticipated by the players and supporters alike. Keflavik could hardly be described as attractive opponents, but even then considering our recent performances in Europe a crowd of just over 13,000 for the first leg at Easter Road was extremely disappointing. At that time the Hibs fans had been accustomed to seeing plenty of goals in European games, and had probably turned up expecting another rout. If that was the case then they were to be disappointed with only a 2-0 home win. With Jim McArthur still injured and McKenzie ineligible, Bobby Robertson was again between the posts. As we expected Keflavik played nine at the back making it very difficult for us, their blond goalkeeper Olafsson in particular pulling off two saves from Pat Stanton and Jimmy O'Rourke that could only be described as in the miraculous class, but like the supporters we were extremely disappointed not to have scored more. Keflavik had been shown up to be what they were, very keen part-timers who rarely threatened Robertson, and it already appeared that a rare goal by centre half Jim Black and another from Tony Higgins would be more than enough to see us safely into the next round. On a personal level I didn't enjoy the game. On receiving the ball I was usually instructed to ping long diagonal cross-field passes to either O'Rourke or Edwards on the right which meant, with so much possession, most of our play was down that side of the park, leaving me at times a virtual spectator.

The return leg turned out to be far more difficult than we could have imagined. My main memory of the trip was the long coach journey from the airport to Keflavic through a desolate wilderness of lava fields sparsely populated by only the occasional wooden house. The game itself took place on a freezing cold early evening in front of a very poor crowd of less than 4,000 on an atrocious muddy pitch covered in places by huge puddles. It was possibly the worst surface any of us had ever encountered, which is really saying something considering that some of us had played on public parks like the Gyle and Inverleith. We fell behind to a goal in the first half when centre forward Zakarriasson scored from a corner, but there was never even the slightest chance of an upset, the second period quite literally shooting in practice for us. Once again we found goalkeeper Olafsson to be in outstanding form pulling off several brilliant saves to deny us equalising on the day, but he could do nothing to stop Pat Stanton scoring from close range after an Alan Gordon free kick had been blasted into the box. It was Pat's fourth goal in the past few weeks making him Hibs' top marksman during that period. Unusual for a European tie there was no after match reception, and we made our way to the airport immediately after the game, just pleased to be going home.

With so many top class sides in the UEFA Cup, our hopes of avoiding one of the favourites were dashed when we were drawn against Leeds United in the next round. At that time Leeds were a daunting challenge. Since the last meeting of the sides in 1968 the English side had won the UEFA Cup twice, the League championship, both the FA and League Cups, and would go on to win the championship again at the end of the season. We had been going quite well ourselves but at that time we lay in sixth place in the league table. The legendary former Leeds centre half Jack Charlton had written us off in a newspaper article with the advice that we should save ourselves the expense of the bus travel from Edinburgh, advice as you can imagine that made us all the more determined to leave Elland Road with a good result. After our pre-match meal at the hotel I watched the well-known television commentator Barry Davies go over photographs of the Hibs players with Eddie Turnbull. It seemed to me that outside of Rangers and Celtic the English TV pundits had little knowledge of Scottish football, perhaps guilty of thinking that Great Britain ended at Berwick.

Once again we were instructed by Eddie Turnbull to attack from the start and it's fair to say that we surprised our more illustrious opponents. Leeds, who had a well-deserved reputation for rough and intimidating play set their stall out early when inside the opening few minutes the rugged Terry Yorath tackled Alan Gordon with, as one newspaper report later put it, 'criminal intent', and we were all amazed, probably even the Leeds players, when the referee simply ignored what should clearly have been a penalty and possibly even a sending off. The incredible decision only served to make us all the more determined and although I say it myself, the midfield trio of myself, Alex Edwards and Pat Stanton were in top form, completely dominating the proceedings. Although a first half effort by Lorimer did give us a scare, only a fantastic display by the Leeds and Scotland goalkeeper Dave Harvey prevented us from taking a one or two goal lead into the interval. Tony Higgins, who had become something of a regular in recent weeks missed the best chance of the game late in the second half when he shouted for Alan Gordon to leave a cross from the right. Unfortunately, Tony appeared to mistime his jump and his header flashed over the bar. I could not believe it as it seemed so much easier to score, but despite our dominance, in the end both teams were happy to settle for a no score draw. In the dressing room after the game we were all delighted at playing so well against what was perhaps the best side in England, although the boss was understandably disappointed that we had not scored at least a couple of goals. Our performance, if not the result, had given us great confidence for the second leg at Easter Road. After the game Jack Charlton conceded that we had fully deserved to win having 'murdered Leeds in midfield' and had particular praise for Pat Stanton. After the game Eddie Turnbull met up with his former Famous Five colleague Bobby Johnstone who apparently could not believe just how well we had played.

Still buzzing from the performance at Elland Road we met Rangers in the first leg of the League Cup at Ibrox a few days later and were much the better side until Schaedler scored another spectacular own goal – Erich rarely did things by half – when he headed past the surprised McArthur. Alex McDonald, always the consummate sportsman, was warned by the referee for his 'overzealousness' in congratulating the Hibs defender. I always disliked playing against McDonald. In direct contrast to the Rangers captain John Greig who I always found hard but fair, McDonald was a particularly sly and nasty player, well capable to my mind of getting up to unpleasant antics.

In the return leg against Leeds at Easter Road we faced an injury weakened side, although they could still call upon players of the calibre of Reaney, Bremner, Lorimer, Clarke, Jordan and Eddie Gray, so they were clearly going to be no pushovers. It turned out to be a really good game played at a good pace and I felt that we had again done ourselves justice but just could not break down a determined Leeds rearguard that was fantastically marshalled by Billy Bremner. Playing in the unaccustomed role of sweeper Bremer dominated the later part of the proceedings, sometimes taking us on all by himself. I have to say that the Scotland captain was quite superb throughout, although his supreme arrogance and gamesmanship often infuriated the large partisan home support. I was guilty of missing a couple of chances to give us the lead, but the big talking point came early in the second half when Alan Gordon scored what appeared to be a great headed goal, only for it to be ruled out for offside. The TV cameras later showed the referee's decision to be wrong, but after a hard fought 120 minutes of goalless action it was on to penalty kicks, the first time either of the sides had faced the situation in a competitive game.

Pat Stanton missed the first of the penalties that were taken at the 'Dunbar' end of the ground when his otherwise well struck shot hit the post. All the remaining players were successful, my own effort a left foot shot into the left top corner of the net, and after our valiant efforts over the two legs we were devastated to be making an exit from the cup under these circumstances. As you can imagine the atmosphere in the dressing room after the game was subdued, everyone extremely disappointed after our Herculean efforts, not just at the defeat but also at the thought of letting down the fans who had turned up in huge numbers and had given us fantastic encouragement throughout the game. The boss was also visibly down, but told us that we had been unfortunate not to win the game and at least we had shown everyone just what we were capable of. Perhaps the stats say it all. As an indication of our almost complete dominance of the game, five of our attempts on goal had been cleared from the line, and as well as hitting the post and having a goal wrongly disallowed, there had been numerous desperate saves by both Shaw, and Letheran who replaced the young goalkeeper late in the game. After the game Billy Bremner was complimentary:

> Hibs are a brilliant team and I can't praise them enough. They did everything but score. If luck had been right for them they would have won by three or four goals and we could not have complained.

I knew some of the Leeds players from playing for Scotland, and several of them came up town with us for a few drinks after the game. Although they all offered their commiserations there was little that could be said in the circumstances that could have repaired the hurt of such a disappointing result.

We later learned that Don Revie had infringed the rules by standing in the centre circle along with the players as the penalty kicks were being taken. Tom Hart immediately complained to the UEFA representative at the game, and flew to Switzerland in the morning in an attempt to overturn the result, but unfortunately to no avail. Revie would later be found guilty of a deliberate infraction of the rules and fined, although Hibs' attempts to overturn the result ended in failure. Bizarrely, although Hibs had technically won the case, they were still required to forfeit their deposit.

The return leg of the League Cup fixture against Rangers at Easter Road was unusual for the fact that for the first time in many years the game took place in the afternoon. Industrial action by electricity workers had meant that surprise blackouts were likely to take place at any time, and in the interests of safety all evening games had been prohibited. There was a welcome return for John Brownlie who was playing only his second game since breaking his leg almost 11 months before, but despite the cavalier performance of the highly rated defender, a no score draw saw us making an exit from the competition. Rangers had come to Edinburgh totally committed to protecting their lead from the first leg, and with most of us playing well below our best they were successful in their aims.

Surprisingly, although we were still sitting in fourth place, a 2-0 win against St Johnstone at the end of November was our first away win of the season, the goals predictably scored by the prolific partnership of Alan Gordon and Jimmy O'Rourke as I again watched from the bench. I had had a very poor midweek game against Rangers, failing totally to get to grips with Greig and Jackson in midfield and probably deserved to be dropped, although I felt I had been no worse than some of the others who kept their place against St Johnstone.

However, I was back in my usual position of inside left in time for the New Year derby at Easter Road. That afternoon Hearts were celebrating the start of their centenary year, and I celebrated the occasion by scoring both goals in a 2-0 victory, this time trying to keep well away from Alan Anderson. According to the *Evening News* I had given what was described as: 'a scintillating performance', adding:

> It is no secret that a number of representatives from English clubs were at the match to cast an eye over Alex Cropley, and this outstanding performance did his potential move to England no harm.

My first goal was scored from an acute angle near the byline. After being forced wide to evade a tackle I simply hit the ball low and hard across goal and was fortunate to catch the goalkeeper, who had anticipated a cross, off his line. But, even if I say so myself, the second was a real beauty. Every player knows instinctively when they have struck the ball well, and my 20-yard drive screamed past Kenny

Garland to bring the house down.

At the end of January Eddie Turnbull motored south to sign Joe Harper from Everton. Joe had played under Eddie at Aberdeen before his move to England the previous season and it was no secret that the boss was a huge admirer of a player who had usually been the top goal scorer wherever he had played. At that time there was a fantastic team spirit at Easter Road and it was no secret that we all thought that the signing of Harper was unnecessary, his inclusion seeming to upset the equilibrium of the side. We were also well aware that someone was likely to go to make way for Joe, possibly Jimmy O'Rourke, leaving us to wonder if this was just the start of wholesale changes. For me the side had at least another year left in it, but Turnbull would later tell me that he had to think about the long term future of the team. With all due respect, as far as I was concerned most of the team spirit went out the window when Joe arrived. Because of their previous relationship he would call the manager by his first name instead of the time honoured 'boss' like the rest of us, and we started to watch our backs, things not as carefree as they once had been. We were also convinced that Joe was on more money than the rest of us, although this was later disputed by the manager who rejected the claim, but this could easily have been worked around with the signing on fee. I didn't dislike Joe, but I wasn't enamoured with him as a player. Alan Gordon was an intelligent leader of the line as opposed to Harper who was more direct and far from being a team player, who often played for himself. Joe Baker had also been a great goal scorer but nobody could argue that he didn't play for the team. At Aberdeen, Davie Robb had done most of the running while he scored the goals. I think that Joe thought he could do the same at Easter Road, and I didn't really enjoy playing alongside him. He had a great eye for a goal and was fast over the first few yards, but he was not a great trainer and in my eyes didn't work nearly hard enough.

Harper was still serving a two match suspension from his time at Everton and he made his debut in a dull and dreary no score draw at Falkirk, the biggest cheer of the afternoon reserved for Alan Gordon when he replaced Harper late in the game. It was only too obvious that Joe was carrying a bit of weight and he would spend the next few games on the bench.

As if to prove that the manager hadn't needed to sign the former Everton man, Alan Gordon and Jimmy O'Rourke, thought to be among the favourites to be replaced by Harper, both scored hat-tricks in the coming weeks, Alan Gordon's in an exciting 3-3 Scottish Cup draw with Dundee at Easter Road. In the midweek replay at Dens Park, described in one newspaper as a 'Nightmare at Dundee', we crashed out of the cup with hardly a whimper as Dundee wrapped the game up in a 15-minute spell in the first half when they scored three goals. It was a terrible display in front of a huge travelling support that had made its way from Edinburgh. It must have been. My dad who always stayed to the end, decided that he had seen enough of 'this rubbish' midway through the second half and stormed out of the ground, my mum following closely behind.

It was around that time that I was given the opportunity to resurrect my international career with a surprise call up to the Scotland Under 23's set-up by manager Willie Ormond, for a European Championship match against Wales at Pittodrie. Watched by a number of English managers including Dave Sexton of Chelsea, I lined up alongside Rab Prentice of Hearts who was winning his first representative honour in a 3-0 win against a much weakened Welsh side. Our goals were scored by Parlane from the penalty spot, Robinson and a counter from St Johnstone's Jim Pearson in the very last minute, but once again the Scottish press had been kind to me:

> The tenacious and creative Cropley was easily the best of our midfield trio and if any one of the Scots impressed the posse of watching English managers it would be the Hibs inside forward.

The newspaper article must have done the trick and a few weeks later Pat Stanton, Erich Schaedler and myself were all called into the Scotland squad for the friendly against Germany in Frankfurt. Although I had missed the game against Holland because of the injury received against Belgium, except for a few Under 23's games I had been overlooked for well over a dozen internationals since, including the qualifiers for the World Cup finals that were to be held in Germany that summer, and was convinced that the opportunity of playing for the full international side again had passed me by. Although disappointed at being overlooked, it hadn't really bothered me all that much and I just wanted to get fit and continue to do my best for Hibs. The game, a 2-1 defeat against the country of his father's birth, turned out to be Erich Schaedler's first and last for Scotland. It was also to be Pat Stanton's 16th and last game for the full international side. In what was a personal nightmare for the Hibs captain, he conceded a first half penalty, and was clearly at fault for the second goal when he was dispossessed in midfield. I was on the subs bench but was not called upon. None of us would play for the full side again.

Joe Harper scored his first goal for Hibs in a 3-3 draw with St Johnstone on the Saturday, finally ending the season with 11. Alan Gordon scored his fifth and final hat-trick for the club in a 3-0 win over Dumbarton at Easter Road a few weeks later, his second was Hibs' 100th of the season in all games. It was a surprise to us all to say the least when Pat Stanton was dropped for the game to be replaced by Gerry Adair who was making a rare appearance since his signing from West Bromwich Albion at the end of the previous season. Stranger still, the club captain was not even on the bench. It was well known among the players that Pat and the manager did not see eye to eye, but this was perhaps the first public indication that all was not well behind the scenes.

Since the signing of Joe Harper I had managed to figure on the score sheet seven times, twice from the penalty spot. During the same period Jimmy O'Rourke had notched four, and Alan Gordon ten including two hat-tricks, so it was a huge surprise when the tall former Hearts player was not included in the line-up for the last game of the season against Dundee United. There was an even bigger shock for the fans when it was revealed after the game that Gordon had been put on the open to transfer list along with centre half Jim Black. Black had been an ever present since losing his place because of injury, first to Gerry Adair and then Derek Spalding, ending a run of 112 consecutive games, so Jim being put on the list was perhaps a bigger surprise than Alan Gordon who's place had perhaps been in some jeopardy after the signing of Harper.

Despite scoring well over 100 goals in all games, Hibs ended the season in second place to Celtic who were winning the championship for the ninth consecutive season, four points behind the leaders and only one point ahead of third placed Rangers. It was the first time the club had finished in second place since the days of the Famous Five in 1953. However, our inconsistency, particularly the points dropped against teams below us in the table, now made me seriously question my future at Easter Road. In the final game of the season, a 4-1 victory against Dundee United at Tannadice, the Chelsea manager Dave Sexton was in the crowd to see me score Hibs' first goal after only two minutes, although by now the secret was out and even the newspapers were declaring that Arsenal were the favourites for my signature.

CHAPTER EIGHT

A Dream Move to Arsenal
and Leg Break Nightmare

DURING THE SUMMER both John Blackley and Erich Schaedler had been selected for the Scotland squad that made its way to Germany for the World Cup finals, John playing against Zaire, while Erich had to be content with a seat in the stand for the entire tournament. Once again there had been no place in the squad for either Pat Stanton or myself, but by now I more or less expected to be excluded. Since I had last played for Scotland almost two and a half years before, Kenny Dalgish had firmly established himself in the side as had Willie Morgan of Manchester United, Archie Gemmill of Derby County and the Leeds United trio of Joe Jordan, Eddie Gray and Peter Lorimer, making a place for me even more remote.

Back at Easter Road Jim Black, who somewhat ironically had just been voted player of the year by the Hibs Supporters' Association, was still on the open to transfer list, as was Alan Gordon and Jimmy O'Rourke, the latter on the list at his own request. O'Rourke and Gordon had finished the previous season as the club's top goal scorers, and for me this was yet another indication that things were not as they once had been. Jim Black would soon rejoin Airdrie, his place at Easter Road taken by young Derek Spalding. Dundee-born Spalding had come through the youth system at Easter Road and was a decent player. Although he was not as tall as Jim Black he was very good in the air and had more pace, but I thought he was more one for the future. It was obviously now a time of great change at Easter Road, the manager in the process of rebuilding the side, and I was now more determined than ever to get a move to England.

A three game pre-season tour of Norway ended with two wins and a draw including a 3-1 win against Rosenborg, and we were somewhat surprised to discover on our return to Edinburgh that we had just been drawn against the Norwegian side in the first round of the UEFA Cup.

But first things first. Although we were all desperate to retain our hold on the Drybrough Cup, this time we found Rangers to be a much tougher proposition than before, and we were beaten 3-2 at Easter Road after defeating the newly promoted Kilmarnock 2-1 in the opening round. It was our first loss in the competition in eight games. At one stage against Rangers we had been three goals behind, until two late strikes by Joe Harper gave us some hope of saving the tie, but try as we might we just could not force an equaliser and very reluctantly we relinquished our two year hold on the trophy.

By this time Joe Harper had gone some way in convincing us that Turnbull had possibly been right in signing him from Everton. Joe had already scored five goals from five starts including the pre-season games in Norway, but in a friendly against Nijmegen at Easter Road he would go a step further by scoring all five in a completely one sided 5-0 victory. He still jokes that he must be the only player in history to score five goals in a game and still be booed from the field by his own supporters. But the fans weren't booing Joe, they were cheering the introduction of the immensely popular Alan Gordon who received a rousing reception when he replaced the former Aberdeen player late in the game. I don't think that Joe was ever the most popular player at Easter Road, especially with the fans who held him responsible for breaking up the great striking partnership of O'Rourke and Gordon. I also felt that Joe himself was not too happy at Hibs, and although he would score several important goals during his two and a half seasons at Easter Road he would move back to his great love, Aberdeen, in 1976.

In a tough League Cup section that included Dundee, St Johnstone and Rangers, we managed to qualify for the quarter finals for a fifth consecutive season, winning five of the six games, the only setback a 2-1 defeat at Dens Park. On the morning of the opening game against Rangers at Easter Road, Jim Black rejoined his former club Airdrie for a fee around £8,000, the papers that morning also full of stories regarding a proposed move to Chelsea for me. A few days later Jimmy O'Rourke was transferred to St Johnstone, making, as so often happens, his debut against his former club. As could be expected Jimmy received a great reception from the Hibs fans who had made their way to Muirton for the game, which was a fitting tribute for the 12 years he had spent at Easter Road, and particularly for his recent prolific goalscoring partnership with Alan Gordon.

One day during the summer I had been surprised to be contacted by Eddie Turnbull who asked me to come to chairman Tom Hart's luxury house in the west side of the city the following morning. I arrived to find Eddie Turnbull, Tom Hart and the Chelsea manager Dave Sexton already at the house. It was immediately obvious from the demeanour of both parties that the club had already agreed my transfer to the London club. Chelsea, who were then in the middle of a rebuilding programme having just signed David Hay from Celtic and John Sissons from West Ham, were offering me far more money that I was on at Easter Road and the security of a three-year contract, but the major drawback was that Sexton needed an answer right away. Although I was hugely flattered at the interest, I explained that I didn't think I was in a position to give him an answer at that particular time and the negotiations came to an abrupt end. Probably having been tipped off by someone at the club, somewhat prematurely several newspapers were reporting that evening, that I was set to join Chelsea for a club record fee of £170,000, some even stating that I would be on £50 per point, that added to crowd bonuses could easily make my weekly wage as much as £200 per week.

Although there had been no recriminations on Hibs' part, it now seemed obvious that Ian Munro had been signed earlier as my direct replacement. At that time Tom Hart had invested a considerable sum of money in the club, and it was perfectly understandable that he would be looking to get some of it back.

I was now married and living in a house in the Willowbrae area of the city. The wedding had taken place earlier in the year at Barclays Church in Bruntsfield with all the first team players in attendance. My wife Liz was well aware that a footballers life could sometimes mean moving around the country, and after telling her of the approach from Chelsea, to her credit she simply replied: 'It's your job; if that's what you want, go for it.' My dad, however, thought that it was a great opportunity for me, as did my brother Tam who encouraged me to get away from Easter Road as soon as possible as he could already see the team starting to slide. I myself was ready to move, but not to Chelsea.

Although it was not public knowledge at the time, I had already been in contact with Arsenal for well over a year. Their Scottish scout had visited the house several times to confirm that the Highbury club were extremely keen to sign me, and there had also been regular telephone calls and the occasional meeting in town. At first I found the interest from Arsenal exciting, but after a few months when nothing much seemed to be happening I put the whole affair to the back of my mind to concentrate on doing my best for Hibs. It later turned out that the major stumbling block had been Eddie Turnbull. Arsenal's chief scout Gordon Clark, a former teammate of my dad's at Aldershot, had made several trips to Edinburgh to see the Hibs manager but had been totally rebuffed. Clark would later tell me that Eddie Turnbull was possibly the most ignorant man he had ever encountered in his life, and he would regularly telephone me at the house to complain that all Turnbull did was swear at him. Now, however, it was obvious that Hibs were prepared to sell me, and immediately after the meeting with Dave Sexton I contacted Arsenal who urged me strongly not to sign anything, reiterating that they definitely wanted me but for some reason could make absolutely no headway with Hibs.

I don't know if it was Eddie Turnbull's way of showing his displeasure at my turning down the move to Chelsea, but I spent the next few weeks warming the subs bench before I finally regained a first team place, this time at inside right, either Ian Munro or Alan Gordon filling my regular position on the left.

I scored my first goal of the season in Hibs' 1-0 League Cup victory against Rangers at Ibrox, and two the following week in a 3-2 win at Pittodrie. The second was a simple tap in after good work by Harper who had already scored with a stunning 20-yard free kick, but I was really pleased with the first. According to one report:

> Cropley's first goal against the Dons won't be bettered throughout the season. It was a solo classic from the moment he collected a short pass from Alan Gordon in the centre circle until he crashed an angled left footer past Bobby Clark from ten yards, a goal that couldn't have come at a more appropriate time since Hibs had struggled up to that point.

Three goals in two games is a great return in anybody's book, but I was extremely disappointed not to figure on the score sheet against Hearts seven days later. I had a good record against our rivals from the other side of town but this time Garland managed to save my effort from the penalty spot and another from Joe Harper a little later, although we did manage to keep up our good record against them intact with a 2-0 win. Apart from the 4-1 defeat at Tynecastle the previous season Hearts had now failed to beat us in the league for well over six years.

The 3-1 victory against Roseborg during our pre-season tour suggested that we would have no difficulties against the Scandinavian part-timers in the first leg of the UEFA Cup in Norway, and so it proved, although the result was slightly closer this time around. Leading 2-0 at half time I scored what was Hibs' 100th goal in European competition, to give us what we all thought to be a commanding lead. Centre forward Iversen thought differently with two late goals that according to us should never have been allowed. At the first he shoulder charged the goalkeeper into dropping the ball before netting, the second when he was allowed to slip the ball past McArthur in the final minute despite appearing to be almost five yards offside. Although the linesman had immediately raised his flag the referee allowed the goal to stand much to our fury. To give the official his due he apologised to us in the dressing room after the game explaining that he had not seen the linesman's signal, but against a much better side his poor decision could well have had more serious consequences.

Although I wasn't aware of it at the time, both the Arsenal manager Bertie Mee and chief scout Gordon Clark had been among the Easter Road crowd to watch me in action in a comprehensive 4-1 victory against Kilmarnock in the quarter finals of the League Cup. I had a particularly good game that evening scoring one of the Hibs' goals, and was later told that the Arsenal pair had left the ground raving about me. It had been the first game under the new vastly improved Easter Road floodlights, although according to one newspaper report the next morning: 'once again Alex Cropley had been the shining light of the evening'. Although they were heartening words, I tried never to make the mistake of letting the headlines go to my head.

A few days later I was again contacted by Arsenal, who urged me to try to get things moving from my end. For some reason they were still having no luck whatsoever with Eddie Turnbull who simply rejected any approach out of hand, and it was difficult to work out why if the club had been willing to transfer me to Chelsea, why they were so vociferous in rejecting any approach by Arsenal. The only thing that I could possibly think of was that as a player Eddie had once been on the receiving end of a humiliating 7-1 defeat by Arsenal in a friendly at Highbury in 1952, but even that seemed much too simple an explanation. After much deliberation I decided that I would have to take the bull by the horns and approach the boss directly, but even this was much easier to say than do. A few days later I summed up the courage to go up the stairs to his office but even then I was so full of trepidation that I had great difficulty in even knocking on the door. Eventually I managed to summon up what little composure I still had left, and entered the office to find myself facing a stony faced Turnbull who demanded to know what I wanted. I was so overcome with nerves that the words simply wouldn't come out, and it was left to him to break the ice by asking: 'You want more money don't you?'. I just nodded. I had long suspected that several of the other players were on more money than me, possibly Pat, and almost certainly Joe Harper, and I felt that I should be at least on the same as them. 'Leave it with me' Turnbull growled, and at that the meeting was over. I never did hear any more about it, but perhaps it was the catalyst behind my move from Easter Road a short time later.

In the return leg against Rosenborg at Easter Road, I scored twice from the spot as we ran out easy 9-1 winners. It was Hibs' biggest ever victory in a competitive European tournament. As the scoreline would suggest it was all too easy against the part-time side and we gave them a real doing. Played during a thunderstorm, Rosenborg stunned us by taking an early lead with a great curling free kick to level the overall score, but the end result was never seriously in doubt and at half time the game was all but over as we left the field 5-1 in front. Although I had missed from the spot against Hearts I was not lacking in confidence, and after Munro had been brought down in the box, I managed to grab the ball before Joe Harper could get to it, and proceeded to dispatch it past Thunshelle in the Rosenborg goal without any bother. Late in the game I scored another from the penalty spot after John Brownlie had been fouled in the box, Pat Stanton completing the scoring with a header in the final minutes.

At that time things were going well and we were scoring goals for fun, particularly in a 6-2 defeat of Motherwell when we were simply unplayable. We had also reached the final of the League Cup after Joe Harper had scored the only goal of a drab game with a fantastic 25-yard drive against Falkirk at Tynecastle. The victory set us up almost predictably with yet another meeting with Celtic in the final, but although we were not to know it at the time, the wheels were about to come off the wagon in spectacular fashion.

At the start of what would turn out to be a disastrous eight days for the club we travelled through to Glasgow for a cup final rehearsal with Celtic and were absolutely murdered 5-0. Although we were once again up against a very good Celtic side, we were absolutely woeful on the day, just a pale shadow of a side with any championship aspirations, and were perhaps lucky to get away from Parkhead with just five. Most of the damage was done in a nine minute period in the first half when we conceded three goals, and a fourth just after half time finished the game as a contest. Possibly as a portent of things to come, centre forward Dixie Deans had scored a hat-trick and we simply didn't have an answer, the comprehensive victory giving the home side a great psychological boost before the cup final at Hampden seven days later.

In a midweek game at Easter Road we had the misfortune to come up against a very good Juventus side who were more than capable of scoring goals, leaving me to wonder why Italian football at that particular time was normally so defensive and negative. In the tunnel before the game I remember looking across at the Italian players to see by what can only be described as a collection of giant Greek, or in this case Roman, gods. With their slicked back hair, swarthy skin and fantastic upright physique, they certainly looked the part and I knew that it was going to be a difficult night.

Roared on by a huge crowd of just under 30,000 we started the game well but found Juventus to be just that yard quicker, and eventually we struggled against their quick counter attacks. Joe Harper missed a great opportunity to give us the lead midway through the half, but we were perhaps fortunate to go in at half time only one goal behind after Gentile had opened the scoring only two minutes before the break. I felt that personally I had done quite well, as had Pat Stanton and Derek Spalding who were both immense at the back, but the big difference between the sides was the aging but still brilliant Brazilian superstar Altafini, who had come on as a second half substitute. We equalised midway through the second half when Pat Stanton scored with a header from a great Edwards cross. I put us ahead a few minutes later when I lobbed the ball over the great Dino Zoff after an Arthur Duncan shot had come crashing back off the bar, but from then on it became the Altafini show as the veteran dominated the remainder of the game with his accurate passing and lethal shooting, scoring twice himself and setting up another. Although he was mostly playing at the other end of the park from me, at times I could only stand back and watch in admiration as he displayed his incredible skills, and it was perhaps no disgrace in losing to such a talented side, who were rightly applauded from the field at the end by the Hibs supporters, who were aware that they had just witnessed a team at the very top of their game. We took absolutely no consolation in going down to what was Hibs' heaviest ever home defeat in Europe at that time, and we now had a mountain to climb if we hoped to overturn the result in Italy.

The big games were coming thick and fast and we took the field against Celtic in the League Cup final at Hampden on the Saturday, a game that probably came far too soon for us after the hugely disappointing defeats of the past few days. Despite an inspiring team talk from Eddie Turnbull I felt that we went into the game lacking in confidence and our defence never really got to grips with Celtic's free scoring forward line, particularly Dixie Deans who scored yet another hat-trick. With Alex Edwards and Ian Munro playing well we still had a chance when we went into the break only 2-1 behind after Harper had pulled one back just before the interval. Joe managed to score another twice in the second half, but his goals could not prevent another embarrassing reverse and we eventually went down 6-3, the worst defeat in a League Cup final since Rangers had lost 7-1 to Celtic in 1957. Joe Harper had proved a constant menace in the Celtic penalty area throughout the entire 90 minutes, and there cannot be many players who have managed to score a hat-trick in a national cup final and still end up on the losing side. As the players trooped dejectedly into the dressing room after the game, a clearly devastated Eddie Turnbull told us that all we could do was forget about it, there was nothing else for it.

I had played my part in the humiliating results of the past few days, and although it might seem mercenary, to me the cracks had started to widen and the recent embarrassing defeats only reinforced my determination to leave Easter Road.

I scored what would turn out to be my last ever goal for the club in a 5-0 defeat of Morton a week after the cup final. The result did little to ease the pain of the previous few weeks, and as can be imagined we came nowhere near in the end to overturning the 4-2 deficit in Turin, finally going down 4-0, and 8-2 on aggregate.

In Turin Erich Schaedler, Arthur Duncan and Pat Stanton had been our top performers, and with any luck Pat might well have scored a couple in the first half when we had more than held our own. In the second half a magnificent overhead kick by centre forward Anastasi gave Jim McArthur no chance and the Italian side a two goal lead on the night, and the writing was on the wall.

On Saturday 30 November I lined up against Ayr United at Easter Road. We were lying third in the table at that time and the hard fought 2-1 victory kept us in contention in the title race. Ayr fought tigerishly, sometimes over robustly, for a share of the points and nearly succeeded until Pat Stanton scored the winner from a Duncan cross with just six minutes remaining. Although I wasn't to know it at the time, it would turn out to be my last ever game for Hibs. The Hibs side that day was:

MCARTHUR, BROWNLIE, AND BREMNER; STANTON, SPALDING AND
BLACKLEY; SMITH, CROPLEY, HARPER, MUNRO AND DUNCAN.
(SUBS) SCHAEDLER AND MURRAY.

As we were getting ready for midweek training at Hunters Hall, Alan Gordon happened to mention that although it had not yet been announced in the press it was no secret that Ally MacLeod had been signed from Southampton the previous day for around £25,000, adding that the club had to sell me now as they would be needing the money. As we were warming up I saw Eddie Turnbull striding across the field towards me. Nothing much was said only that Arsenal had come in for me if I was interested. I was driven to Easter Road to change where we were met by chairman Tom Hart before all three of us made our way to Turnhouse to catch the plane to London. During the flight the atmosphere was cordial with nothing much said about the potential transfer, only that it could be a big move for me.

At Heathrow, Arsenal had booked a private lounge and we met manager Bertie Mee to discuss terms. For me the move had nothing at all to do with money, but as well as a three-year contract plus a three-year option, Arsenal were offering to more than double my wages. At that time I think I was on about £70 per week at Easter Road, the Arsenal deal worth around £150 per week plus another £30 appearance money. It had all seemed so long since I had first been contacted by the Arsenal scout that I had begun to think that it was never going to happen. Hibs accepted Arsenal's offer of £150,000, and after that everything happened so incredibly quickly, like a whirlwind. It didn't take me long to accept the Highbury terms and I returned home that evening with Tom Hart and Eddie Turnbull not even having left the airport.

At Easter Road Eddie Turnbull wished me all the best as did Tom Hart, but having agreed to return to London the following day

I regretted that I had not had time to say goodbye to the players, some who had since become great personal friends. There was one slight downside to the deal. I mentioned earlier that the move south had nothing to do with money, but as Hibs were receiving £150,000 for a player who had cost them nothing and had given them several years loyal service, I felt that I was at least due something from the transaction. Hibs stubbornly refused to budge even after Bertie Mee had a word with them on my behalf, and I have to admit that it did leave a slight taste in my mouth.

Looking back, perhaps I should have made the move much earlier. I had loved every minute of my time at Easter Road, playing with such a great bunch of lads, but had felt for some time that maybe we had had our moment and that it would probably be all downhill from here. Several talented youngsters such as Bobby Smith, Willie Murray, Lindsay Muir, Alec McGhee and Lawrie Dunn, had all started to break into the first team squad, but I don't think Eddie Turnbull was as comfortable in dealing with the youngsters as with the more experienced players, and was sometimes found to be dogmatic and lacking in patience. Eddie's man management skills often left a lot to be desired, and it is well known that many of the younger players didn't get on with him, something that may have eventually led to his own downfall and Hibs' relegation at the end of the decade.

Any speculation as to who would make way for new signing Ally MacLeod was dispelled later that evening when it was announced that I had signed for Arsenal. MacLeod was an extremely talented player with a good touch and a good football brain. Although a bit on the slow side he more than made up for it with his reading of the game. Ally had first come to prominence when scoring all of St Mirren's goals in a 4-0 defeat of Rangers, at Ibrox of all places, a couple of years earlier. Rangers as was their habit at the time of signing any player who had played particularly well against them, immediately tried to sign him, but he had elected to move to Southampton in a deal worth £40,000 instead. For some reason it had not worked out for Ally in England, and currently on loan at Huddersfield he was pleased to be joining Hibs, resisting a late attempt by the then St Mirren manager Alex Ferguson to lure him back to Paisley.

Alan Gordon would soon join me out the door at Easter Road. Alan had scored what turned out to be his last goal in his final appearance in a Hibs jersey in a 1-1 draw with Dunfermline at East End Park a few weeks before. After turning down an earlier move to Motherwell, the immensely popular Gordon joined Dundee a few weeks later to become one of the very few players to have played for all four Edinburgh and Dundee clubs. His transfer now meant that only around half a dozen players remained at Easter Road from a side that had popularly become known as Turnbull's Tornadoes.

I returned to London on the Thursday and the following day was collected from my hotel in Southgate by the Arsenal physio Fred Street and taken to meet my new teammates at a light training session at Highbury before making our way to Carlisle for the next day's game. I must confess, I found entering the foyer at Highbury for the first time a daunting experience. To see the bust of Herbert Chapman, the famous marble staircase and the mosaic of the gun laid out on the floor of the reception area was a truly emotional experience, and I had a mental image of the many famous players who had crossed the mantle throughout the years. The ground itself was fabulous, the pitch, complete with a first class undersoil heating system which was then pretty rare in the game, in tip top condition. There was also a huge club shop run by the legendary former Arsenal and Wales goalkeeper Jack Kelsey, and the row of buses used by the lesser sides all neatly parked side by side outside the stadium, left me with no illusions that I had joined a really big club.

Bertie Mee had been a player with Derby County and Mansfield Town before the war until suffering the serious injury that was to end his career. After training as a physiotherapist he had joined Arsenal in 1960 and was somewhat surprised to be asked to replace manager Billy Wright in 1966. Under Mee, Arsenal had won the Fairs Cup in 1970, the clubs first silverware for 17 years, the famous double in 1971, and had been losing FA Cup finalists the following year. Although they still had the nucleus of the double winning side, they had ended the previous season in 10th place in the table and exited the FA Cup at the first hurdle to second division Aston Villa at Highbury, form that was not nearly good enough for a club like Arsenal. Having just signed both Brian Kidd and goalkeeper Jimmy Rimmer from Manchester United they were then in the middle of a major rebuilding programme.

I didn't know any of the players personally, although there were plenty whose faces I recognised, but they all made me more than welcome, particularly Eddie Kelly who hailed from Glasgow. Kelly was a terrific lad, very easy to get on with, and a great laugh. Pleased to meet a fellow Scot he took me to lunch that afternoon and we remained great friends during my time in London. Perhaps surprisingly, I didn't really have any nerves. I knew that I was a good player and that I had come from a really good side so I didn't envisage any problems. I found manager Bertie Mee to be a really nice fairly placid man. A couple of the players had their own issues with him while I was at the club but as far as I was concerned he was always fair and encouraging, and was well liked by the majority of the staff. I have to say, though, that discipline at the club was sometimes found to be wanting, as demonstrated when Eddy Kelly threw his jersey at the bench after being substituted in a game against Newcastle, a situation that just would not have been tolerated at Easter Road.

I don't think that Bertie really knew all that much about the tactical side of the game but had the sense in the early days to surround himself with people who did, like Dave Sexton then manager of Chelsea, Don Howe then with West Bromwich Albion, and later Keith Burtenshaw and Bobby Campbell. With his portly physique I always thought that the manager always looked slightly ridiculous in a tracksuit, and he reminded me of the famous film director Alfred Hitchcock. I can still visualise Bertie jumping to his feet after Charlie George had scored with a fantastic 30-yard drive during training with the cry: 'Oh-La-Lah', leaving the rest of the players in stitches.

As Ally MacLeod was making his first appearance in a green and white jersey as a second half substitute in a no score draw against Airdrie at Broomfield on Saturday 7 December 1974, I was making my debut for Arsenal in a 2-1 defeat at newly promoted Carlisle. Playing wide on the left instead of my more accustomed midfield role, I found the pace of the game to be no faster than in Scotland, and in fact found I had more room and time on the ball. The tackling could be just that little bit crisper, but I was well capable of looking after myself on that score. At Arsenal the style was very different to what I had been used to, the emphasis more on team work than individualism. At Hibs I had been encouraged to go from penalty box to penalty box, but now I was told to keep behind the ball at all times, the main object being to get it to the big man up front. During the second half against Carlisle a huge fight involving most of the players had broken out after a particularly bad tackle. Brian Kidd, who had a short temper at the best of times, was immediately into the middle of the fray. I could only stand by in bewilderment as the police entered the field to break things up, and for a while all I could make out were police helmets flying all over the place before order was eventually restored. A clearly embarrassed Bobby Campbell later apologised, adding that things were not always like that. Although I had what can only be described as a quiet debut, I had enjoyed it, and was in for the long haul... or so I thought at the time. The Arsenal side that day was:

RIMMER, RICE AND MCNAB; KELLY, SIMPSON AND MANCINI;
STOREY, BALL, RADFORD, KIDD AND CROPLEY.

As my new teammates were making their way back to London after the game, I travelled back to Edinburgh with my mum and dad in order to put things in order before my wife Liz and I made the journey back to England during the week. Arsenal had made arrangements for us to stay in a hotel in Southgate until the club house we had been allocated at Hadley Wood, at a rent of £9 per week, had been decorated.

At that time I was well aware of the adverse effect the bright lights of the big city had apparently had on the career of my former Hibs teammate Peter Marinello a few years earlier. Peter had failed to live up to expectations at Arsenal before his move to second division Portsmouth, but that didn't bother me in the slightest. The bright lights held little appeal for us. Both Liz and I were home birds who preferred to stay in at night and watch TV, with only the occasional wander around Southgate, and the even rarer trips into the centre of London.

At that time Arsenal were a pretty ordinary side and quite clearly a team in transition. Although they still had some very good players, several from the double winning side, it wasn't quite happening for them and only a few weeks before I joined they had been rock bottom of the table, ironically after a 2-0 defeat by rivals Tottenham, their eighth loss from the opening 13 games. Not long before, the popular Ray Kennedy, who had formed such a prolific partnership with John Radford up front during the double winning year, had been allowed to join Liverpool for £200,000. Kennedy would prove to be the legendary Liverpool manager Bill Shankly's last ever signing for the club, and has since been described as the final piece in the jigsaw of a great Liverpool side. Ray had been Arsenal's top goal scorer in the double winning season and a regular contributor since, and many considered his transfer to be a major setback in the rebuilding process. Kennedy's striking partner John Radford was still at the club and was some player. Probably because he was such a big strong lad he wasn't all that quick, but he was a great target man, didn't shirk a tackle and was very good to play alongside. As a person John was not all that outgoing, a bit quiet, and I found it quite difficult to get to know him. At that time he was nearing the end of his career and most of his close friends were from the double winning side. When I first arrived at Highbury, World Cup winner Alan Ball appeared to be the main man although there was resentment among many of the players over the fact that he was allegedly being paid much more that the rest. Ball, a powerful personality who liked to be the centre of attention, was a super player who never gave any less than his very best. With the fire he had in his belly, I always felt that he should have been a Scot, a compliment no doubt that would have repulsed the fiercely patriotic Englishmen. Ball hated losing and would often end up with tears of disappointment welling up in his eyes after a defeat. He was a good captain who would gee you up by shouting and bawling, as opposed to the Hibs captain Pat Stanton who would be much more composed, taking the time to explain things, but both men were great captains in vastly different ways.

I quite rated Pat Rice, who was a very determined competitor. Although his distribution could have been a lot better, he was a winner, a good tackler and he would run all day to help the cause. A great servant who would spend the majority of his playing career at Highbury, Pat would later go on to play an important part in Arsenal's fantastic success, as a coach under Arsene Wenger until his recent retirement from the game because of illness.

In those days all the top teams had a hard man whose rugged style of play would simply not be tolerated today. Chelsea had David Webb; Leeds: Norman Hunter; and Liverpool: Tommy Smith. At Arsenal we had Peter Storey. Peter had a reputation as a hard man but at times I didn't think that he was all that hard, sometimes cowardly, kicking people from behind. He was, however, an extremely good passer of the ball and a fiercely committed player, but had some strange sayings and it sometimes took me a while to understand just what he was talking about. Nicknamed 'snoutie' by the rest of the players he would occasionally also be called 'Gerse' after the Brazilian Gerson on account of his fantastic passing ability.

Eddie Kelly and Sammy Nelson became my best pals at Highbury and we would often go for a drink together after games. Eddie was a great lad with a fantastic sense of humour. He was another very fine player and had been the first substitute to score in an FA Cup final during Arsenal's victory over Liverpool in 1971. Sammy Nelson and I also got on extremely well. A typical Irishman who could be loud at times but exceptionally funny, he seemed to know everyone in London, and he would often take me golfing or into town to meet some of his many friends.

At that time Peter Simpson was one of the older members of the side. Another great passer of the ball and a player who could really tackle, Peter was quick over a short distance, his long legs helping him to make up the ground, and without doubt he would have won many more England caps had it not been for Bobby Moore – he was that good.

When I first moved to Highbury, Charlie George was in dispute with the club, although I never did find out why. A great talent but very temperamental he also had an issue with Alan Ball, and I remember once during training when he deliberately went over the top, Ball only managing to evade serious injury by his sharp reactions. Quick and with great ability for such a big man, Charlie was as sharp as a tack and great in the air. His ongoing dispute with Bertie Mee and injury meant that we would play only a few games together before his eventual transfer to Derby County.

At the beginning of the season my fellow Scot, Bob Wilson, had retired from the game after well over 300 games at Highbury to further a career in broadcasting. Bob's replacement, Jimmy Rimmer, was some machine. A very good goalkeeper who worked tirelessly at his trade, he was a great trainer and would practice endlessly during the afternoons on the sandpit saving balls from some of the younger lads. He was a great shot stopper, but frankly I found him to be something of a weirdo. I suppose it's a well-known fact that most goalkeepers are as 'daft as a brush' and Jimmy could possibly be described as a truculent eccentric. He lived only a few doors away from me, but although he wasn't a bad lad, he wasn't someone that I would choose to go on a night out with. Ironically, I would later have a small part to play in his move to Aston Villa. During one game Sammy Nelson and I were watching from the stand when Rimmer received what looked like a serious injury. A stretcher was immediately called for and as he was being carried from the field, apparently in some distress, he suddenly jumped to his feet and ran back to take up his position between the posts. Sammy and I just looked at each other and burst out laughing.

Brian Kidd lived just over the way from me and was another that I got on really well with. Living so close we would often go out for drinks together in Southgate, but Brian would normally only call at my house when it was dark in case he was seen by Jimmy Rimmer who would want to come along with us. Brian never really settled in London. After his move to Arsenal his wife remained in Manchester, Brian commuting back at weekends, a situation that was later to play a big part in his move to Manchester City. A big strong lad who took no nonsense, I found the former Manchester United and European Cup winner good to play alongside. He linked up well alongside John Radford in a 4-4-2 system, with both myself and Alan Ball playing in the hole behind the big front men.

In defence we had Terry Mancini. Terry had been signed from Queens Park Rangers as a direct replacement for Frank McLintock on the recommendation of coach Bobby Campbell. At Loftus Road he had been something of a legend but he was another player that I considered to be not nearly good enough for Arsenal. With all due respect to Terry he would later be described by one former Arsenal player in an autobiography as 'someone who would not have got within miles of the Arsenal team a few years earlier', and he would not be at Highbury long before a move to Aldershot on a free transfer.

At that particular time the club also had some very good young players. Graham Rix, David O'Leary, Frank Stapleton, David Price and Brian Hornsby. All were keen to learn and would soon break into the first team. Hornsby was a quality player but unfortunately he lacked heart and would become very much a reserve at Highbury until his move to Shrewsbury in 1976. Liam Brady, though, was a fantastic prospect. At just 17 years of age he was so good that he just could not be held back any longer. For someone so young he had great awareness and a huge desire. With a wonderful left foot he just ghosted past players and reminds me today so much of Jack Wilshere. Liam was a lovely quiet lad who would soon be taken under the wing of Alan Ball, and who could have asked for a better mentor to further your football education than Alan Ball?

One person I haven't mentioned yet is George Armstrong. Long serving 'Geordie' was a great favourite with the supporters. By then getting past his best, some Arsenal fans are under the impression that I was brought in to replace Armstrong, but although George could play on either wing, during my time at Highbury his normal position was wide on the right while I played either wide left or left midfield. A great crosser of the ball, with a particular talent for dangerous in-swinging corners, George could run all day. During his 16 years at Highbury he would play well over 600 games, and it was with great sadness that I learned of his premature passing from a brain haemorrhage in 2000 aged just 56.

As I have already mentioned at Arsenal I found the training to be disappointing. So repetitive, mundane and lacking in imagination it was a far cry from what I had been used to at Easter Road, although admittedly the Hibs manager was a very difficult act to follow. Bertie Mee took little to do with the training itself preferring to leave that side of things to Bobby Campbell and the other coaches, but he was always there in the background watching the proceedings. The training facilities at the London Colney College however were second to none and a far cry from some of the facilities that I had been used to at Hibs. Another major difference compared to Scotland was the treatment and concern for the players. At Highbury we were all cosseted and made to feel extra special. Nothing was too much trouble with even the slightest whim immediately attended to, and in the dressing room we even had our own thick red dressing gown and slippers, although it did take me quite a while to get used to the luxury of the underfloor heating.

On match days we would meet for our pre-match meal at South Herts Golf Club where the famous Welsh golfer Dai Rees was the professional. Sadly Dai, who was a great Arsenal fan, would succumb to the injuries received in a car crash in 1983 on his way back from watching a game at Highbury.

After a game most of the married players would normally just have a quick beer in one of the lounges then go straight home, far different to what I had been used to in Edinburgh where several of the Hibs players would usually go for a few drinks at the popular White Cockade pub in Rose Street where we would mingle with the fans.

On the weekends when we didn't fly back to Edinburgh to visit our families, Liz and I would like nothing better on a Sunday morning in Southgate than to go for a walk if the weather was nice, often stopping to watch the cricket on a local green.

At Highbury, travel to the away games was very different from what I had been used to. Probably because the distances were normally that much greater, the club had its own luxury coach fitted with all mod cons including a small kitchen with two chefs, a TV, and even several beds for the players to relax in after a particularly gruelling game.

One slight problem I did encounter after moving to London was the language barrier. Not only did I occasionally struggle with the many different accents I sometimes failed completely to understand just what they were talking about. For instance, if someone put a great ball through, Peter Storey would describe it as a great 'pill', and for some time I would hear the players in the dressing room discussing someone called Bertie. For the love of me I couldn't quite work out who this Bertie was and it was only later that I discovered that they were talking about the manager. Out of respect I would simply call Mee 'Boss' and I found it slightly disconcerting to hear most of the other players address him simply as Bertie, a familiarity I had not been accustomed to at Easter Road.

Although the game itself was no faster than I had been used to in Scotland, down south most of the teams were far better organised and every game was a challenge. The better players were also far better thinkers, and were often quite capable of giving you the run around as I found out in one of my early games against Chelsea when I discovered Alan Hudson to be in a different class. Hudson was a real handful and quite literally I never even got a kick of the ball all afternoon. There were so many difficult opponents including George Best and Geoff Hurst and you had to be on top of your game at all times. Most were also fierce competitors and you just couldn't afford to relax for a moment. In one of my early games for Arsenal against Stoke City, I was lining up in the wall to defend a free kick when fellow Scot and former St Mirren player Jimmy Robertson stamped really hard on my foot as if to say 'Welcome to England'.

I scored my first goal for the club in the return league game against Carlisle at Highbury when I managed to prod the ball over the line after a melee in the goalmouth, John Radford later telling me that I had the heart of a lion. According to one newspaper report:

> Nobody could grudge Cropley his first Arsenal goal since his £150,000 move from Hibernian. He got in where it hurts – to the heart of a seething wall of bodies and flying feet to bundle home a winner which could prove priceless to the once mighty Arsenal.

The goal, the winner as it turned out in a 2-1 victory that eased our relegation worries, was all the sweeter for me as both my mum and dad were watching from the stand.

The first round of the FA Cup had thrown up a home tie against lower league side York City, newly promoted from the third division. A 0-0 draw at Highbury left the newspaper reporters salivating at the prospect of a famous cup upset, but in the replay at Bootham Crescent we all played well to defeat the second division side, my own particular performance helping even more to cement my move to London. Although I had been particularly happy with my performance that afternoon, trouble lay not too far ahead.

After just seven games for Arsenal, on Saturday 18 January 1975 we travelled north to face Middlesbrough at Ayresome Park. On a softish pitch that may well have had something to do with events, I managed to just nick the ball away from the Middlesbrough defender Stewart Boam who accidentally caught me just above the ankle with his toe. The referee awarded us the foul and although the leg felt a bit numb I thought no more about it and managed to play on, the game ending 0-0. After the game my wife and I headed straight back to Edinburgh for the weekend. There seemed to be no reaction from the leg and I forgot all about it. It was only after taking part in a small sided midweek game on the shale pitch behind the clock end of Highbury that I felt a soreness. The next day at training it felt really bad and physio Fred Street advised me to bathe it in the hot tub. On arriving back home after training I had the strangest feeling that all the leg needed was a good stretch and I started to sprint from my car to the hotel entrance. I had only gone a few yards when I heard a loud crack and collapsed in utter agony, barely managing to make it to my room. I immediately phoned Fred Street who came to the hotel. Thinking that it was no more than ligament trouble he strapped up the leg, but unfortunately a deep scan at the hospital the following morning revealed that it was broken, though fortunately for me it was only the fibula which is non-weight bearing, and a clean break.

The next few weeks were spent in plaster although I could still manage to shuffle around, and the long and monotonous road to fitness began all over again. After the removal of the plaster I was able to do light body exercises and also managed to make a few visits home to Edinburgh, but there was one down side. As the treatment progressed I was instructed to wear a huge laced up boot with a low heel that had been designed to support the leg and ankle. It seemed to be about a size 13 and looked more like a clowns shoe, so you can well imagine the ribbing I took from my friends.

Later I would run alongside the second team physio while Fred watched from the side-lines. Street, who was also physio to the England team, and I believe related, either through descent or by marriage, to the famous Rothschild family, supervised my treatment throughout. Although he was very good at his job, I don't think he came anywhere near to providing the same nurturing devotion as Tom McNiven at Hibs.

I later discovered that the injury was so unusual that Mr Vardy, the Spurs physio, wrote a medical paper on it. In Vardy's view it was the training that had caused the stress on the bone, the injury perhaps exacerbated by the hot baths.

On one of my visits back to Edinburgh during my recuperation, Arsenal had phoned ahead to ask if I could take part in some light training at Easter Road. Hoping to catch up with my former teammates, I was disappointed at arriving at the ground to find that the players were training elsewhere so I just covered some laps of the pitch and several runs to the top of the huge terracing, nothing strenuous just to work up a sweat. Eddie Turnbull came out to see me and we exchanged pleasantries. Everything was cordial, just general enquiries about how I was finding things in London. I knew that it was nothing personal, but Eddie sometimes had a habit of spitting while he was talking, and as I stood there resplendent in my smart Arsenal tracksuit complete with the famous logo of the gun, I remember looking down to see that my trainers were covered in spit. No manager wants to lose his best players and Eddie was kind enough to tell me that it had been a big mistake to let me go, explaining that the decision had been taken out of his hands at a higher level, and was obviously only about money.

During my absence Arsenal would spend the remainder of the season flirting with relegation and at the end of February were 18th in a 22 team league. With three teams now going down we were obviously in big trouble but finally managed to finish in 16th place, the clubs worst position since 1925, which however is more than can be said about Dave Sexton's Chelsea who were relegated along with Carlisle and Luton. An otherwise decent run in the FA Cup ended, when after victories against York City and Coventry that both required replays, and a 1-0 win against Leicester City, we were beaten 2-0 by local rivals West Ham in the sixth round, the Hammers going all the way to the final that year where they would eventually defeat Fulham 2-0.

The injury had meant me missing the rest of the season, or as one newspaper reporter kindly reminded everyone, costing the club around £15,000 per game. I could well have played in the last few games of the season, but with the club now in a more secure position and out of the cups, nothing was at stake and it was decided not to take the risk. Although I had not played in the closing games of the season I had been in full training, and now fully recovered from the leg break I was delighted to learn that I had been included in the party that would make its way on the financially lucrative four game tour of Kuala Lumpar, Penang, Singapore and Bangkok. I have to admit that I disgraced myself on the flight to the Orient. During the 19 hour flight by Trident I more than took advantage of the plentiful supply of free drink available on board, which believe it or not was not like me at all. Things might well have been different if I had stuck to my usual Martini and lemonade which unfortunately had run out, and I continued on Gin, a drink that was new to me. Needless to say I was absolutely guttered, making numerous visits to the toilet to be sick, totally oblivious to the fact that sick bags were provided in front of the seats. I was rough, so bad that I remember my good pal Eddie Kelly motioning to chairman Dennis Hill-Wood: 'Look at him Mr Chairman. 150,000 quid? – he's not worth two bob!'

I played in all four games, managing to score against a Bangkok XI. In Penang we faced a Malaysian Select who were as quick as anything back home and as sharp as a tack. At times, before they later ran out of steam, we just couldn't get near them and at one point Peter Storey became so frustrated that he had to be held back from setting about them by Brian Kidd. The game against a Singapore select was played in a beautiful oval stadium, the pitch as lush as I had played on. Like the Malaysian select they also played football of a good quality before tiring near the end.

Penang and Singapore were lovely cities but Bangkok was an absolute doss house. Not nicknamed sin city for nothing, the place seemed to be full of nothing but massage parlours and various other dens of iniquity. This didn't prevent some of us from looking around however, and a group including the club doctor Mr Crane visited the famous, or infamous, tourist attraction Boogie Street, where many of the bars had tables outside on the pavement for the dancing 'girls', to display their wares. The Doc, who was a very respectable family man, got absolutely pissed, and was absolutely mortified when we informed him the next morning that the beautiful girl he had been dancing with had actually been a man.

By this time Liz had given birth to my daughter Jennifer who was born at Barnet Hospital. Jennifer was a welcome addition to the family, but by now Liz was acutely homesick, missing her family badly. Often she was so depressed that it was an effort just to get out of bed in the morning, and although this didn't stop her from caring properly for the baby, unfortunately her unrest was worsening by the day. We tried to get back to Edinburgh as much as possible with the baby, normally every two weeks or so, living with Liz's parents in the Tollcross area of the city, but in the end even this did little to ease her unrest. Being fairly quiet she had not managed to make many friends in London, although Jimmy Rimmer's wife Cathy was often around, and I suppose that its understandable that a young woman with a new baby would want to be surrounded by her family.

CHAPTER NINE

Terry Neill, More Leg Break Heartache and Life at the Villa

THE PRE-SEASON TRAINING at Highbury was no better than normal. Hugely disappointing, mundane, uninteresting and lacking in variation, and was not remotely in the same class as I had been accustomed to in Scotland. At our training camp at London Colney everything seemed to consist mainly of running and other unimaginative exercises, although we did have a couple of closed door games against Nott's County and the local side Barnet. People will possibly be fed up hearing it, but nobody could come even close to being as good or inventive as Eddie Turnbull at Hibs as far as training is concerned.

Afterwards, we made our way to Scotland by coach for warm up games against Hearts, Dundee and Aberdeen. In those days the roads were not nearly as good as they are now and the journey across the border seemed to take forever. I can still remember an exasperated Eddie Kelly shouting to the driver: 'how long is this going to take driver, we've gone through darkness twice already?' In Edinburgh we stayed at the Post House Hotel which gave me the opportunity to catch up with John Young who had been the best man at my wedding, my pal Mike Collins and my former Hibs teammate Jimmy O'Rourke who was then running the Corstorphine Inn on the west side of the city. A 0-0 draw against former rivals Hearts at Tynecastle was followed by a game against Dundee at Dens Park, during which I managed to score. The main talking point after the game however had been the performance of a 17-year-old red headed player called Gordon Strachan who had been absolutely fantastic. Head and shoulders above everyone on the pitch, even that early he looked destined for a great future in the game. I have since been told that Gordon had been on Hibs' books as a provisional signing during my time at the club, but had been released by Eddie Turnbull after a dispute with his dad. Sadly, it would prove to be Hibs' great loss.

We approached the new season with high hopes, thinking that surely things couldn't be as bad as the previous campaign, but a 1-0 defeat by the newly promoted Bristol City in the opening game soon dispelled that notion. The defeat was an almighty blow to our confidence and ultimately it would prove to be yet another dreadfully disappointing season for the club and its supporters. By now Alan Ball, Peter Storey, George Armstrong and Peter Simpson were all over 30. The talented youngsters coming through such as Liam Brady, Frank Stapleton, David O'Leary and Graham Rix were not quite ready, and they often failed to receive the help they were entitled to expect from some of the more experienced players who were often found to be struggling themselves.

There were some bright points however. At Highbury early in the season we faced a very good Manchester City side that would go on to win the League Cup by defeating Newcastle United in the final at Wembley. Although they were not the great side of a few years earlier, they still had players of the calibre of Joe Corrigan, Willie Donachie, Mike Doyle, Dennis Tueart, Joe Royle and my old roommate Asa Hartford, and remained formidable opponents. Leading 2-0 at the interval, another goal by Rodney Marsh seconds after the restart seemed to have all but secured a victory for the away side, but we responded magnificently with a spirited fight back. Alan Ball scored with a great 30-yard screamer. Another by myself a short time later when I slipped the ball past Joe Corrigan gave us renewed hope, but unfortunately, try as we might, we just could not manage the equaliser that perhaps our spirited performance deserved. One newspaper article described the fight back:

> Cropley capped a great display when he fastened on to a slick Alan Ball pass to slip the ball past the advancing Corrigan. Three goals down after 46 minutes, everybody played their part but Arsenal's magnificent rally owed much to the performance of the midfield trio of Cropley, Ball and Brady.

The result fell far short of the victory that was desperately needed with us again in a precarious league position, but the spirited comeback had given both the team and the supporters real optimism for the future. In October there was a satisfying win against Coventry, four of our five goals scored in the first half, two by myself, two by Brian Kidd, the other coming from Alan Ball. If the victory against Coventry was satisfying, on a personal level scoring the winner against Middlesbrough two weeks later in what was my first appearance against the Teesside club since breaking my leg against them nine months before, gave me far more pleasure.

Although the victories had been satisfying the truth is that I was not really enjoying my football at that time. I had featured in almost all of the opening 18 games of the new season, missing only one. In a 3-1 defeat at Birmingham around mid-November I took a knock and was replaced by John Matthews. Once again I thought no more about it thinking it was nothing more than a slight strain, but during the week the leg continued to trouble me and a scan later revealed what was an extremely rare injury; my left fibula had a crack running up the leg instead of across as would normally be expected. Told the only cure was rest, I would not play for the first team again for several months, and once again I was left to face the long and dispiriting period of boredom while I worked myself back to full fitness laterally with games for the reserve side.

A week after a 2-0 defeat by Spurs at Highbury, on 10th April I was recalled to the side for the first time in over four months in a 0-0 draw against Everton at Goodison. I was selected for the remaining four games of the season, but overall as well as it being for me personally a disastrous campaign, it had turned out to be another very disappointing season for the club. Beaten 3-0 in the FA Cup by a very poor Wolves side, morale at Highbury at that time was at rock bottom and we finally finished 17th, one place lower than the previous season. Overall our performances had been very poor, victories rare, and with the team once again languishing in the lower half of the table attendances had more than halved and something had to be done. Rumours had been doing the rounds for some time regarding Bertie Mee's future at the club and during the close season the boss was sacked, a move that probably came as no surprise considering recent results. Mee was no fool, and even he would probably have known that his coat had been hanging on a 'shooglie peg' for some time. For a while there had been whispers that the former Arsenal defender Terry Neill would be taking over from Mee, and in mid-July his appointment was made public. The former Northern Ireland international Terry Neill had been a huge favourite with the fans during his 11 years at Highbury until his move to Hull City in 1970. After a spell managing Hull and two seasons with Arsenal's great North London rivals Tottenham Hotspur, he was welcomed back to Highbury not only as the club's youngest ever manager, but almost as the returning messiah. A typical brash Irishman with the gift of the gab, at times I thought that Terry tried too hard to be loved by everyone. He was another who in my opinion knew very little about the game, and I didn't particularly like the man.

Apparently, when Bertie Mee had been offered the Arsenal manager's job in 1966, he had been so unsure of the promotion that he had asked for assurances that he could get his old job as physio back if things didn't work out. As far as I am aware the obviously deeply disappointed Mee never set foot in Highbury again, at least not while I was there.

The new manager brought in Wilf Dixon as first team coach, making Bobby Campbell surplus to requirements at Highbury, and he would soon take over from Alec Stock as manager of Fulham. I had rated Bobby who was a good talker and always tried to motivate the players, although some of the things he said were quite obviously rubbish. Once after a game in Kuala Lumpar, he told me that even Johan Cruyff wouldn't have attempted a pass that I had completed, which I knew was complete nonsense. I got on quite well with Wilf Dixon who was an old teammate of my dad's at Aldershot, but again as far as I was concerned he was too old, devoid of ideas, was yet another that didn't really know the game and unfortunately I don't think he ever quite got the players behind him. The players are always the first to discover when someone isn't quite up to the job and it didn't take us long to suss Wilf out.

One of Terry Neill's first moves was to bring in Malcolm McDonald, a free scoring centre forward from Newcastle for a then British record fee of £333,333. Again, maybe I had been spoiled by playing alongside some of the best but I never really fancied Malcolm as a player. He was unbelievably quick, scored goals for fun, but was all hash bash with no subtlety. He could sometimes appear to be brash, loud and a bit full of himself but deep down was really a nice enough guy. I often roomed with Malcolm, liked him a lot, and it was a great pity when he announced his premature retirement from the game due to injury at only 29 years of age.

Terry Neill had his own particular ideas regarding training and during a pre-season trip to Yugoslavia and Switzerland he had us all up at 6am for a pre-breakfast run before we got down to the actual training. Considering that we were all spoiled footballers, most of us were totally unaware that there was even such a thing as six o'clock in the morning, and it's an understatement to say that the early runs were not particularly popular with the players. Neill's coaching style was part functional and part method, but unfortunately he fell far short of the game when explaining just what he wanted from his players.

For me personally, things really came to a head after a game against Grasshoppers in Zurich when the manager accused me of not trying. I may sometimes have played badly but nobody could ever have accused me of not trying, something that was totally alien to my nature, and I was far from happy. After demanding an immediate meeting with Neill, the manager was all bluster without really saying anything, certainly falling far short of anything resembling an apology. His hurtful and untrue comments made me dislike him even more, and for me the writing was now on the wall regarding my future at Highbury.

Just before we made our way to the continent, my good pal Eddie Kelly also had a major fall out with the manager this time over a minor training incident. It was all over something quite trivial, but I believe the underlying problem was also Kelly's deep dislike of Neill and he would soon be on his way to Queens Park Rangers.

Back at Highbury I was now playing far left in a four man midfield with Liam Brady taking my usual position. Out wide you tended not to see as much of the ball and I disliked playing there. I could see what Terry Neill was trying to do with Brady playing alongside Alan Ball in the hole behind the front two, which to be fair to the manager was a good pairing, and if I am honest if I had put my mind to it I could probably have done much better than I did on the flank. I had my doubts however, both regarding my position in the side and also about the manager. Neill knew that I was unhappy and had lost a bit of interest, but he completely ignored the situation. Had Bertie Mee still been at the club he would undoubtedly have had a word with me regarding my concerns, which to my mind is good man management, something that was sadly lacking in Terry Neill.

I turned out for Arsenal against West Ham at Upton Park on Saturday 11 September 1976 in front of a 32,415 crowd when goals from Trevor Ross and Frank Stapleton were enough to give us a 2-0 victory. It would be my last ever game for the club.

ARSENAL: RIMMER, RICE AND NELSON; ROSS, O'LEARY AND HOWARD; BALL, BRADY, CROPLEY, STAPLETON AND ARMSTRONG. SUB: STOREY.

For some time now I had been in the habit of visiting the Arsenal chief scout Gordon Clark at his home for a chat. Gordon was particularly friendly with Bertie Mee and was another who had absolutely no time for Terry Neill. He had known for a while that I was unsettled at Arsenal and had promised to do all he could to help me get a move. Meanwhile we had been drawn away against Preston North End in the League Cup. By then I was really unhappy at Highbury and was concerned that if I was selected against Preston that I would be cup-tied, a move that could potentially hinder any possible transfer. The day before the game I again visited Gordon's house and I was taken aback when he asked what I thought about a move to Aston Villa. I was still determined to prove myself in England and wasn't keen on going back to Scotland at that particular time, so the possibility of a move to Villa really interested me. Gordon immediately got Ron Saunders on the phone. Saunders was very affable, putting absolutely no pressure on me, simply stating that he had a great bunch of lads and was highly optimistic of doing something with them. It was really all small talk, but he had already stimulated my interest in a move to the Midlands. I had played at Villa Park the previous season when Arsenal lost 2-0, and had found them a young workman-like side playing with great energy in front of a fantastic crowd, and I had been suitably impressed. Only later did I discover that I had been recommended to Saunders by the Chelsea manager Dave Sexton who had advised him that I was one well worth following up. Unknown to me Saunders must also have been in touch with Terry Neill to discover that he would have no objections in me moving to Villa Park.

The following afternoon as Arsenal were preparing for the game against Preston, Neill called me over to say that he had spoken to Aston Villa who were interested in signing me and that I could go and speak to them if I wanted. Hurried arrangements were made for me to travel to Birmingham that afternoon and I was met at New Street Station by the chief scout Tony Barton. Villa, who had beaten the holders Manchester City in the previous round, had a League Cup tie against Norwich City later that evening and I was introduced to the players in the home dressing room before the game. While I was in the dressing room the door literally barged open and Andy Gray swaggered in with a cursory 'alright' in my direction with hardly a glance. We had played against each other several times in Scotland and I thought to myself: 'what a big headed sod'. Little did I realise that Andy and I would soon become the best of friends.

I later watched from the dugout as Villa defeated Norwich and was extremely impressed, not only with the stadium itself, but also the fantastic playing surface and the huge crowd, particularly at the Holte End of the ground which was packed to the rafters and making an incredible noise. I remember Andy Gray scoring a fantastic headed goal from a cross from Brian Little in the 2-1 victory, and was particularly taken by the young Gordon Cowans who was playing that evening in my preferred position in the midfield. It didn't take me long to realise that Villa were a very useful side, young and quick. They also played the game the way I thought it should be played, and I was immediately sold. Arrangements were made for me to return to the ground the following morning, and any remaining doubts regarding the move were quickly dispelled when Saunders explained that not only did he want me to make the team play, he also wanted me back into the Scotland set-up. That did it for me. There were no complications, and without the presence of anyone from Arsenal whom I presume had already agreed the move, I signed on the dotted line and the deal was done. In those days there were no agents. You simply accepted or rejected the signing terms that were offered and that was that. Arsenal had lost £25,000 on their original transaction, but the £125,000 paid by Villa made me their second most expensive signing after the £175,000 paid to Coventry for Dennis Mortimer in 1975, beating the £100,000 paid to Dundee United for Andy Gray.

So, after a little under two years at Highbury, during which time I had played 29 league games, 47 in all, scoring 11 goals, once again I was on my way into the unknown. Looking back, only professional difficulties had caused my unrest at Highbury. It was a fantastic club with a great staff. To have played for them was an immense honour, and I am proud to have been associated with such a hugely respected and admired side as the Arsenal.

Meanwhile, Brian Kidd had been another regular visitor to Gordon Clark's house. Brian had been homesick in London for some time, missing his family who had remained in the Manchester area. Disillusioned, he was actually at the point of giving up the game altogether until helped by Gordon, and he too would soon be on his way, in his case a £100,000 move to Manchester City.

Arsenal had already sent my boots up by rail so that very afternoon I trained with the rest of my new teammates at Villa's training ground at Bodymoor Heath. I have to say that my wife wasn't overly happy at the thought of a move to Birmingham, but perhaps selfishly, I was so keen to get away from Highbury that I didn't even discuss the move with her. Villa had put us up in a hotel, where we would spend the next eight months until the house we had bought in a new estate was ready. Living in a hotel wasn't exactly an ideal environment to bring up a kid and both Liz and Jennifer started spending more and more time back in Edinburgh with her folks. I would go back to Scotland as often as I could, Liz coming down on the occasional weekend, but in time her visits to Birmingham would become rarer and rarer.

I have kept one of my first interviews as a Villa player. It escapes me now what newspaper it was from but under the heading: 'Cropley: The set-up will do me fine', to my mind still makes interesting reading.

Villa's latest signing £125,000 Alex Cropley reckons his new club has the talent to go zooming straight to the top. Cropley, who watched his new teammates beat Norwich on Tuesday night says he is keen to meet the players. 'I think I can do a job with them and I am sure they will help me settle in. They are an extremely talented lot of lads and the potential here is vast. The set-up matches it, and everything is just right for trophies to be won.' In the League Cup match Cropley was keenly aware of just how difficult it is to play against Norwich, particularly at home. They made it tough but Villa still managed to create a handful of chances and could well have won by two or three more goals. One thing that excites Cropley is operating from midfield with the talent in the strike force that Villa will have in front of him. He told me that both Andy Gray and Brian Little are fine players. 'They give a midfield man the chance to shine by running into fine positions to receive the ball. There is also the added attraction of Ray Graydon doing so well on the right giving the attack width.'

I made my debut in a 2-0 victory over Leicester City at Villa Park on the Saturday but almost missed the game. Both my wife and I had decided to spend the morning shopping in nearby Sutton Coldfield. Being new to the area I completely miscalculated how long it would take me to get to the ground and arrived well after the others. Fortunately Saunders accepted my apologies and still included me in the line-up. The Villa fans seemed to take to my whole hearted approach from the very start and I won a penalty in the first half that was duly converted by Ray Graydon past the Leicester keeper Mark Wallington. I joined in the goal celebrations as though I had been in the side for years, and even that early knew that I had made the right choice in joining Villa. Unlike at Arsenal there were no cliques, and

I had been immediately struck both by the happy atmosphere at the club and the players evident desire for success.

Aston Villa had been formed in 1874 by a group of cricket enthusiasts looking for something to occupy their time in the winter. Within 13 years they had won the FA Cup, and it was only after a suggestion by the Aston Villa director William McGregor that the Football League had been inaugurated in 1888, the Midlands club taking its place as one of the 12 founding members. Within a decade Villa had become one of the top sides in the country, winning the coveted double in 1897, and by 1920 they had won both the championship and FA Cup six times. Success could not be sustained however and after relegation for the first time in 1936, the subsequent years would be chequered and at times turbulent. Success in the FA Cup for a record seventh time against Manchester United and the famous Busby Babes in 1957, was followed by victory in the inaugural League Cup final in 1961–62 and a further two losing appearances in 1962–63 and 1970–71. Villa would be relegated to the second division in 1960 and again in 1968 with a further humiliating drop into the third division in 1970. Promoted back into the second division as champions, they had performed poorly during the 1973–74 season and at the end of the campaign manager Alec Stock had been sacked to be replaced by Ron Saunders. Saunders had been a centre forward of some repute, although mainly with lower league sides, and had been Portsmouth's top goal scorer in each of the seasons he had spent at Fratton Park. Appointed as manager of Norwich City in 1973 he had led the side to promotion into the top division for the first time in the clubs history and that year's League Cup final where they would lose only narrowly to Tottenham Hotspur. A short spell at Manchester City followed with another appearance in the League Cup final, this time losing to Wolves. Saunders took over the Villa hot seat in time for the clubs centenary season in 1974, not only leading the Midlands club back to the first division at the first time of asking but also to victory in the League Cup final against his old side Norwich that same season. In doing so he became the first manager ever to take three different clubs to the League Cup final in consecutive seasons.

Ron Saunders must obviously have been doing something right, eventually guiding Villa to double League Cup success and the championship in 1981 before resigning suddenly after a contract dispute just months before the club became only the fourth English side to win the greatest prize in football, the European Cup. To my mind however, he was a lucky manager to have inherited such a talented bunch of young players. John Gidman, Gordon Cowans, Brian Little, Gary Williams, John Deehan and Gary Shaw were already at the club when he arrived and together they would go on to form the nucleus of one of the best sides seen at Villa Park for many years.

Although he was obviously immensely popular with the fans on account of the success that he brought the club, Ron Saunders was a dour and serious man who I don't think really knew how to handle people. One of his big problems was a difficulty in communicating with people, and he would often castigate a player in front of others, when perhaps it would have been better done in private.

To give the manager his due however we were all exceptionally fit, but he was not all that great tactically, the players themselves often working out moves that we would use on a Saturday. His philosophy on the game was also very different to mine, preferring the long ball from back to front, often missing out the midfield completely, although saying that, in Andy Gray he had a player who was absolutely magnificent not only in holding the ball up, but in making runs for others.

As already mentioned, after a slow start I really hit it off with Andy. When I first arrived at the club Leighton Phillips took me under his wing, both of us occasionally going for a few drinks either after a game or on a Sunday afternoon. Leighton was married, and because Liz was frequently back home in Edinburgh, I was often in Birmingham on my own and I soon started to hang out with fellow Scotsman Andy Gray. Andy was an extremely sociable person who really enjoyed the high life and he would always ask me along to parties and other social occasions that he was regularly invited to. I was still very quiet, but to give Andy his due he would always make sure I was okay before mingling with his friends, while I just sat quietly in a corner getting drunk. Being far more outgoing than me I suppose you could say that he treated me more like a big brother.

Soon after arriving at Villa, Andy became a partner in a city nightclub named, for some obscure reason, the Holy City Zoo, which for a while was the place to be. The opening night coincided with a game at Villa Park and with us well ahead at half time, I remember Andy asking to be substituted early so that he could attend the opening. The rest of us went up later and had a great night. Initially the club was very popular with the people of Birmingham, but unfortunately it later got into financial difficulties. Ultimately let down by his partners, I believe that Andy lost a considerable amount of money in the venture.

Andy Gray had been one of Ron Saunders first signings for a then club record fee of £100,000, and was surely the bargain of the season. Great at holding the ball up, he was not nearly as tall as you might think, but was utterly fearless and absolutely fantastic in the air. A strong, mobile and aggressive player, he was great at making front post runs to get on the end of crosses and scored loads of goals for us.

When our new house was eventually built just a few hundred yards from where Andy was then living we would often travel to games together. When he first arrived from Scotland, he too had lived for a while in a hotel, sharing a room with goalkeeper John Burridge. Burridge had been signed from Blackpool just a few months before for £75,000 and was as daft as a brush. While night owl Andy normally caught up with much needed sleep in the mornings, John and I would usually go into training early where I would hit ball after ball at him. A great shot stopper, 'Budgie' was absolutely fanatical about goalkeeping and the stories about him are legendary, including the times he would sit with his goalkeeper's gloves on watching TV, with his flatmate Andy instructed to throw an orange at him at any time without warning. During one of our early morning stints, I cheekily chipped John instead of a shooting as expected, and he went absolutely ballistic, screaming 'you don't do that in a game so don't do it now'. Later in a game against Sunderland, I did chip the goalkeeper and I was not slow in reminding him. John was some man and although completely eccentric he was a very good goalkeeper. While a bit on the small side and not that great in the air, he was as brave as a lion and became a great favourite with the fans. A man of many clubs, later in his career 'Budgie' would win a League Cup medal with my former club Hibernian.

Full backs Ray Gidman and John Robson were already at the club when Saunders arrived from Manchester City. For me the stylish Gidman was the best full back in England at that time and on a par with my old teammate John Brownlie at Hibs, which believe me is really saying something. Although not the bravest, he could run all day, was a great crosser of the ball and had a confidence, according to some, that bordered on arrogance. Capped for England against Luxembourg in 1977, it is amazing that it turned out to be his one and only appearance for the full side. He would later move to Everton before a transfer to Manchester United late in his career.

If I had compared Gidman to Hibs right back Brownlie, then John Robson had the same qualities as the Hibs left back Erich Schaedler.

As a footballer John was as hard as nails, quick and brave. A versatile player who could also play up front, he usually played directly behind me, and if anything got past me then John would invariably be there to mop it up. The holder of a Championship medal won in 1972 playing under Brian Clough at Derby, John at times could be very quiet, but he was a very good footballer, another nice lad, and it was a great tragedy when he succumbed so early in life to illness.

Gordon Smith had joined Villa from St Johnstone shortly before my arrival. In Scotland he had normally played up front, but after John Robson's illness he had slotted into the left back position as if he had played there all his life. Defensively John was the better of the two, but Gordon was quite nippy and often liked a foray up the park. I would often room with him on the away trips. Sometimes we would be given a Mogadon tablet to make sure we had a good night's sleep before a game and I remember once being awakened in the middle of the night by an almighty crash and jumped out of bed to see Gordon standing there swaying in a dazed state after walking into the wall. When asked if he was okay, with glazed eyes he just answered 'aye' before climbing back into bed.

In the heart of the defence captain Leighton Phillips and Chris Nicholl were an ideal back four pairing. Both were as different as chalk and cheese but combined well to create a formidable barrier for opposing forwards. Although he was no slouch, Welsh international Phillips was not all that quick but he more than made up for any shortcomings in that department by his great reading of the game. Playing at sweeper behind Nicholl, he could be a bit hot headed, but was a good talker and brilliant in the air. Leighton's centre back partner Chris Nicholl was a big lad who was totally commanding in the air, but for a first division centre half he was not the hardest. Often he would kick me during our 5-a-side games at training and I would ask him why he didn't do that during a game, but Chris would just laugh. However like the rest of the players he was a great lad and I got on well with him.

Normally Frank Carrodus and Dennis Mortimer would line up alongside me in midfield. Frank was not overly blessed with skill and his passing often left a lot to be desired, but he had great pace and could really cover the ground. After his later move to Manchester City he would be replaced in the Villa side by my former teammate at Hibs Des Bremner, who had similar attributes to Frank.

I had played against Dennis Mortimer with the Scotland Under

23's side before his move from Coventry City in 1975. Like Carrodus, Dennis could also make up the ground from box to box and was great at assisting the front men regularly finding himself in great goal scoring situations. For me however he was far too quiet on the pitch but he had great strength, could pass the ball and was extremely hard in the tackle. He never did play for the full England side but many good judges considered him to be one of the best uncapped players in the country.

Brian Little was another who had come through the ranks at Villa Park. An outstanding talent who was a great foil up front for Andy Gray, Brian had been capped for England against Wales in 1975 when he replaced Mick Channon in a 2-2 draw. Incredibly he was never chosen for the full side again, often kept out by Malcolm McDonald. To me there was absolutely no comparison between the two, but in saying that MacDonald was probably the more dangerous inside the penalty area.

Played wide out on the right wing, Ray Graydon was our out ball. Ray, who linked up well with Andy Gray and Brian Little up front had come through the leagues at Villa since the dark days of the third division, and had scored the only goal in the 1975 League Cup final victory against Norwich. Unfortunately he received a bad injury not long after I joined the club and when fit again found it difficult to re-establish himself in the side and would soon be transferred to Coventry City.

John 'Dixie' Deehan was yet another who had come through the ranks at Villa Park. He only made the breakthrough into the side not long after I joined but soon became a regular. A productive goal scorer who linked up well with Andy and Brian, he would go on to score over 50 goals from well over 150 appearances for the club.

Last but not least Gordon Cowans could certainly play a bit. You could see immediately that he was different class and was going to be some player when he matured. When I first arrived at Villa, Gordon had not long made his debut as a 17-year-old, and was not quite ready for a regular first team place. He was a quick learner though and would make his breakthrough during the coming season, eventually going on to win the League Cup, League Championship, European Cup and Super Cup during his two spells with the club. Later he would become first team coach at Villa Park. Gordon was not only similar in physique to me, but was also a natural left sided midfielder. A great tackler, he was a bundle of energy, tricky and could certainly go past players. His

Dad Walter was our kit man, and whenever I was receiving treatment for a knock on a Friday morning, Walter would pop in to the treatment room to ask how I was coming along. If I said fine, he would simply reply 'that's good son'. If I said I was struggling he would reply 'too bad', knowing full well that my possible omission would make it that much easier for his son Gordon to play the following day.

Part of Aston Villa's secret was that they were mainly all young boys with a great blend of experience. Apart from myself, Andy, Leighton, Chris and John Robson, the rest were all that much younger and were dead keen to learn. Everyone knew each other's play, and similar to my time at Easter Road, there was a great camaraderie both inside and outside the dressing room.

CHAPTER TEN

Yet Another League Cup Final Triumph

THAT SEASON WE had some great early results. I was named Man of the Match in one newspaper after scoring the only goal of the game, with a neat chip against the Sunderland goalkeeper Barry Siddall. Poor Barry was making his debut for a side that would be relegated at the end of the season, and I believe that it was manager Bob Stokoe's last game in charge before his resignation in midweek. Ron Saunders, not a man to give praise lightly told me after the game that the goal had been the best he had ever seen. Exaggerated or not it was certainly one of the best I had ever scored and one that remains imprinted on my mind. A week later we destroyed Arsenal 5-1 in front of a huge crowd at Villa Park. It was my best performance yet since signing for the club. Alan Ball had opened the scoring for Arsenal early on but we were unstoppable on the day and steamrollered the Highbury side into a heavy defeat, a result that obviously gave me great satisfaction. Although I didn't score myself, once again I was lucky enough to be named Man of the Match, our goals scored by Gray (2), Mortimer, Graydon and Little. After just a few weeks I felt really at home, the Villa fans seeming to really take to me. Later in the season there would be an even better result against the reigning champions Liverpool, again at Villa Park. The Annfield side had their full side out that day, Clemence, Hughes, Thomson, Callaghan, Keegan, Heighway, etc., but again we just clicked into top gear from the start and literally blew them away, the Holte End taking great delight in yet another 5-1 victory, sweet revenge for an earlier 3-0 defeat in Liverpool. All the goals were scored in the first half and if I remember rightly both Andy and 'Dixie' Deehan scored a couple, Brian Little the other. David Johnstone scored a consolation for Liverpool. I heard later that the result was so unbelievable that people were phoning the local radio station BRNB from as far away as Australia asking if that really had been the score.

Another game that sticks in my memory but for all the wrong reasons is the friendly against Glasgow Rangers at Villa Park that turned out to be anything but friendly. Rangers had just won the inaugural Scottish Premier League, and with no top team fixtures in either country that weekend on account of international commitments, they were considered a great attraction for a challenge match. I told the rest of the players that the Scottish fans would travel down to Birmingham for the game in droves but they didn't believe me. The night before the game, and in the morning, Birmingham was a sea of blue with several outbreaks of violence creating chaos in the town centre. At one point things got so bad that the police decided to gather up as many of the Scottish fans as they could and herd them into the Holte end of the ground well before kick-off. Things were fine until we went two ahead in the first half and I could sense a change of mood inside the stadium. We were defending a corner in front of the Rangers fans when a bottle landed just feet away from John Gidman. The next thing I remember is 'Giddie' taking off in a flash for the opposite end of the ground and looked up to see the Rangers fans piling over the surrounding fence in great numbers. In no time at all it was complete mayhem with thousands of Rangers fans on the pitch and the referee was left with no option other than to abandon the game as we made for the safety of the dressing room. It was slightly more unnerving for 'Budgie' who had to make his way through the hordes of invaders to retrieve his goalkeeper's gloves, but luckily he escaped unharmed. Nobody likes a smart alec, or in my case a smart Alex, but in the dressing room afterwards I could only sit back and say to the others: 'I told you so'. I had planned to travel back to Edinburgh later that evening, and with hundreds of Rangers fans on the train I sat as near the back as possible in case I was recognised. At every station we passed I could see loads of police with dogs, but fortunately I made it home safely without any altercations.

At that time we were on the crest of a wave, and the games just couldn't come fast enough. We were young, keen, and eager to learn. We also worked hard, trained hard and everything just fell into place. Ron Saunders had a reputation as a hard task master who always produced sides that were extremely fit, but as I have already mentioned he wasn't all that great at the tactical side of the game. Often things would be left to the players themselves. For instance if we were playing a full scale practice match against the reserves, instead of taking things easy as some sides might do, we would try out different things that could be used in games, either two touch or three touch moves. It would all be done amongst ourselves without having to be told and it went someway in helping to mould us into a top class side. The camaraderie at Villa Park at that time was second to none and there were plenty of laughs along the way, although sometimes the victims of our numerous pranks would not always find it funny. One time on an away trip someone sneaked into 'Dixie' Deehan's room and cut a huge hole in his dress tie. Unbelievably, 'Dixie' didn't even notice, and he was preening around the dining room with a huge hole in his Kipper tie, until he was told. As the rest of us collapsed into a heap laughing, the clearly embarrassed Deehan was absolutely furious, although after he had calmed down he later saw the funny side of things.

We were going well in the league, but the highlight of the season was undoubtedly the League Cup run that would see us go all the way to Wembley. I was extremely relieved to have only narrowly avoided being cup tied with Arsenal earlier in the season and I was in the side that faced Welsh side Wrexham in the next round. Third division Wrexham had shocked the football world by reaching the quarter finals of the Cup Winners' Cup the previous season losing only narrowly to eventual winners Anderlecht. They were a good side and in front of another huge crowd at Villa Park they shook us by taking an early lead. This only seemed to give us a jolt and we soon settled. Chris Nicholl scored a rare headed goal from one of my corners to equalise and from then on there was only one team in it. Led by the ever dangerous Andy Gray who scored one of our goals, we played some brilliant stuff, eventually running out 5-1 winners.

After defeating Manchester United 3-2 at home, Andy Gray scoring twice, and Coventry 2-1, we drew 1-1 with both our local rivals West Bromwich Albion and Norwich in the league before facing Millwall in the quarter finals of the League Cup. Millwall were always a stuffy side but a goal from Chris Nicholl and another from Brian Little eased us into a home and away meeting with Queens Park Rangers in the semi-final of a competition that Villa had won just two years before.

Although they would end the season in the middle of the table, at that time Queens Park Rangers were also going very well. Then managed by the former Chelsea manager Dave Sexton they were packed full of quality players, including internationals Gerry Francis,

Phil Parkes, Dave Gillard, Stan Bowles and Frank McLintock. With Dave Thomas, Don Givens, David Webb and John Hollins in the side they also had plenty of experience, and were obviously going to be no pushover. In the first game at Lofthus Road we did well to escape with a 0-0 draw. At times we were really under pressure, failing to create many opportunities inside the opposition penalty box, although I did manage to hit the post in one of our rare forays up the park.

The return at Villa Park was a right good game, nip and tuck all the way, finally ending two each after extra time – John Deehan scoring twice for us, and I think Don Givens had a double for them. The Holte end was packed solid with 27,022 crammed into the traditional end alone, and the atmosphere inside the ground was electric. The thrilling encounter had everything including a penalty save by Burridge from Bob Latchford in the very last minute of extra time, and such was the tension that hardly a soul dared leave the stadium before the final whistle. During the game I was involved in an unsavoury incident with my fellow countryman Frank McLintock. At that time the drainage on one side of the Villa Park pitch was under repair, leaving a damp patch the entire length of the playing area. During the second half I attempted to trap a high ball with the sole of my boot. Unfortunately the ball didn't bounce on the heavy pitch as I expected, and I accidentally caught McLintock on his shin ripping both his tie and sock. To be fair it looked a bad one, and although it was completely accidental it did look as though I had gone over the ball.

Despite my apologies McLintock went completely off his head, grabbing me and calling me all the names under the sun until we were separated by the other players. It was really all handbags but McLintock's protests were enough to get me booked by referee Masterson. In the players' lounge after the game I was called out into the corridor by a couple of reporters who wanted an interview when I was again confronted by a clearly still raging McLintock who grabbed me around the neck, again calling me all the names under the sun including some I had never heard before, and an incident that could easily have got out of hand was only averted by the actions of the newspaper men who stepped in to separate us. Later outside the ground as the Queens Park players were about to board their bus I remember Dave Webb shouting over to me that he was going to send me my stud, presumably referring to my tackle on McLintock. I thought Webb's remarks were rather ironic considering the considerable reputation he had in the game as a rugged defender who didn't take any prisoners, and that's me being kind to him. Whether he was joking or not I don't know, but his remarks annoyed Ron Saunders enough for the boss to reply in the press:

> Alex doesn't want the stud but I'd be delighted to receive it to go with the set of dear old Dave's which I've already had mounted on my sideboard.

I can honestly say that although the tackle may have looked bad at the time, I was not remotely the kind of player to go over the ball, and the whole thing was a complete accident. However it was probably Webb's after match remarks that led to me thereafter being nicknamed 'Studs' by the rest of the Villa players.

In the boardroom after the game the toss of a coin was required to decide the venue for the third game play-off. The story goes that the Rangers chairman Jim Gregory grabbed the coin after it had bounced off the low boardroom ceiling before anyone including the Villa chairman Sir William Dugdale could react, immediately claiming to have called it correctly. Despite protests by the Aston Villa directors; London it was for the third game play off, this time at Highbury.

A 1-0 defeat at Ipswich was not exactly an ideal preparation for the play off, but we travelled to Highbury in good spirits. Once again the game was nip and tuck until we eventually got into top gear, and in the end a Brian Little hat-trick, the first from one of my corners, was more than enough to secure a 3-0 victory and send Villa into their second League Cup final inside three years. Midway through the first half I was blatantly 'done' by Dave Gillard who didn't miss me, the dead leg leaving me struggling and in all kinds of bother. I honestly don't know if it was accidental or not, but at the time I was under no illusions that the tackle was retribution for my earlier altercation with Frank McLintock. Despite receiving a pain killing injection from the club doctor in the dressing room at half time, I was in no fit state to continue and was replaced by Gordon Cowans as I watched the remainder of the game from the dugout.

The atmosphere in the dressing room afterwards was absolutely fantastic, the champagne flowing freely. Ron Saunders was ecstatic, taking it in turns to congratulate each player individually, and it was back to the Baggot Arms in Birmingham, a pub owned by one of the players friends, for a late, extremely late, drunken evening.

The build-up to a cup final in England is vastly different to Scotland.

Down south it is much more of an event. In the weeks leading up to Wembley the Villa players all went round the big companies in the Birmingham area seeking sponsorship for the match programme, the proceeds going towards the players pool. The final also generated far more attention in the press, and as well as being measured for our new club suits that were to be worn on the big day, there was also a boot deal to be negotiated with manufacturers Gola, although in the end most of the players simply wore their own boots that had been doctored by the kit man to resemble that of the sponsor. There was also the appearance money. At the start of each season bonuses are normally built into a player's contract and at Villa it was no different. The club however had obviously failed to take into account us not only reaching the cup final but also the two replays. Ultimately all the players involved received appearance money for each of the games played, a situation if I remember correctly that was quickly changed the following season.

Then there was the big question of match tickets! At Villa all the first team pool were allowed to purchase up to 100 tickets each. The precious briefs were stored in a large walk-in safe at the ground that reminded me of a large bank vault and we would all traipse along to collect them during the week, payment required at the time of purchase. It may sound like a lot, but believe me by the time that family and friends were all accounted for, often there would be very few left. When I was at Arsenal I had heard stories about players from another London club selling their cup final tickets to the famous ticket tout Stan Flashman who would pass the briefs on at a hugely inflated price, one player in particular so I heard, receiving enough to buy a brand new top of the range car. Although it was highly illegal, at that time it was well known that the practice went on, and a blind eye was often turned to it, most of the players considering it a cup final perk.

Before the game we stayed at a hotel in St Albans where we held a light training session on the adjacent pitch. In the morning we met the London press before making our way to Wembley. The journey to the stadium was an unforgettable experience. Just to pass the huge crowds that were making their way to the game, most of them cheering and waving at us, and to see every overpass on the way to the ground festooned with the banners of both teams, was an incredible feeling. I had not been at the stadium before and as we made our way down Wembley Way past the thousands of fans making their way to the game the emotion was almost overpowering.

While taking the time honoured early pre-match walk on the Wembley turf I happened to spot my mum, dad and brother Tam amongst the then fairly sparse crowd inside the huge stadium and that almost did it for me. Unless you have experienced the occasion yourself you cannot begin to imagine just how emotional it can be.

In the immediate lead up to the game the nervous energy in the dressing room was almost palpable, each player going through his own particular pre-match routine, all keen to get going. Before the start both teams were introduced to the Princess Royal and her husband, Mark Phillips. As she passed along the line the Princess spoke to some of the players and apparently asked John Burridge where he came from, to which the bold Burridge answered: 'Somewhere your mother has never been, ma'am, Workington,' which as I recall brought a smile from the Princess. I can't remember her speaking to me, but there is a photograph that appears to show that she did. Looking back, the pre-match formalities were over in a flash but at the time they seemed to take an eternity.

Unfortunately, after all the build-up, there is nothing much that can be said about the game itself except that it has been described as possibly the worst cup final ever seen at the famous old stadium. At the time I didn't think it was all that bad but only realised later after watching the replay on TV that we had let ourselves and the supporters down. After the game both myself and Chris Nicholl were interviewed for ITV by Brian Moore who strongly disagreed with my viewpoint that the game hadn't been all that bad, when he stated firmly that I was wrong; it had been terrible. I tried to make light of it by motioning towards Chris saying that we had been let down by the older players, but by that time even humour was in very short supply.

One of the very few bits of excitement during the whole afternoon had come not long after the restart when the referee stopped the game after being informed that a bandsman had lost part of a spur during the half time entertainment. Despite a cursory search by the players of both sides the offending item could not be found and referee Kew restarted the game. Unfortunately that was the excitement over for the afternoon. The game had been badly in need of a goal and at the final whistle the players of both sides made a half-hearted lap of honour, or as one newspaper put it the following morning, a lap of apology, but by that time most of the supporters had already left the stadium in disgust. In the dressing room the mood was understandably subdued, as was the post-match reception back at the NEC in Birmingham, the flags and banners of congratulations adorning the walls of the hall going some way to create an almost surreal atmosphere.

My mum and dad had travelled all the way down from Edinburgh by car for the game and later complained that the journey had been a complete waste of time, my brother Tam scathing at having come all that way for less than nothing. The newspapers on the Sunday and again on the Monday lambasted the players of both sides. One gave me the Man of the Match award, but the occasion could perhaps best be summed up in Monday's *Sun*, when under the Man of the Match section they had simply written: 'you've got to be joking'. Everton's Duncan McKenzie had suggested that extra time should have been played, leaving the Sun reporter Frank Clough to write: 'for heaven's sake, give us a break sunshine!' Almost everyone was in agreement – the 90 minutes that had already taken place was more than enough for anyone on the one day.

SAT 12/3/1977 ASTON VILLA 0 EVERTON 0 WEMBLEY STADIUM ATT: 100,000
ASTON VILLA: BURRIDGE, GIDMAN AND ROBSON; PHILLIPS, NICHOLL AND MORTIMER;
DEEHAN, LITTLE, GRAY, CROPLEY AND CARRODUS.
EVERTON: LAWSON, JONES AND DARRACOTT; LYONS, MCNAUGHT AND KING; HAMILTON,
DOBSON, LATCHFORD, MCKENZIE AND GOODLASS.
REFEREE: G KEW

The replay at Hillsborough on the Wednesday was better, but not by much. I had picked up a slight hamstring pull during injury time on the Saturday. It didn't seem all that much at the time but it refused to clear up. On the way to the game I still thought that I could make it, but shortly before the start Saunders took me aside to ask how I felt and it was only then that I realised there was no way I could play, and was absolutely heartbroken to miss the game, young Gordon Cowans taking my place in midfield.

Once again even another 30 minutes failed to separate the sides. Villa were leading thanks to an own goal by Kenyon that looked like being enough until Latchford equalised in the very last minute after a melee in the penalty area. Although I was disappointed for the lads, I have to confess that deep down I was secretly delighted to get another chance to pick up a League Cup winners medal to go with the one won with Hibs, and it was on to Old Trafford for the second replay, the only time to date that the League Cup final has gone to three games.

By the time of the third game at Old Trafford almost a month later most of the euphoria surrounding the final had abated somewhat. I

148

had fully recovered from my hamstring pull, but we now had other major injury concerns. Andy Gray would definitely miss the game after picking up an injury in our 2-1 defeat by Derby County the previous Saturday and would obviously be a huge miss. Frank Carrodus would also fail to make it after damaging his ligaments in the same game, and John Gidman was struggling. The doctor had been called to give John an injection just before the game, but unfortunately he was caught up in the heavy traffic making its way to Old Trafford and only arrived at the ground ten minutes before the start with both Saunders and Gidman going absolutely mental. The injection helped but John had to be replaced in the second half by Gordon Smith. As we left the field at half time, my old Scotland boss Tommy Docherty who was then manager of Manchester United whispered encouragement: 'come on Crops, get them playing, get them playing'. Centre half Chris Nicholl had scored the best goal of the game to equalise a first half opener from Latchford, his third in the competition, with a 40-yard thunderbolt in the second half that literally screamed into the net as I ducked. Brian Little gave us the lead a minute later and it seemed that the cup was on its way to Villa Park until Mick Lyon's popped up late on with an equaliser. Once again extra time was needed to settle matters and although we finished much the stronger side, for a while it looked as if the game would again end in stalemate until Brian Little popped up in the very last minute with the goal that won us the cup after a defensive slip up in the Everton penalty area. The former St Johnstone player Jim Pearson, a mouthy individual who liked himself more than a bit, had been niggling away at me all evening, and I have to admit that it gave me the greatest pleasure at the final whistle to pat him on the head and say: 'hard lines, son'.

Nothing could compare with a Saturday afternoon at Wembley, but it was still victory in a cup final, and one that gave us entry into Europe for the second time inside three years. After being presented with the cup and our medals by the Football League President Lord Westwood, we made our way bedecked in scarves and flags that had been thrown on the field by our supporters, on the traditional lap of honour around the Old Trafford pitch, me wearing the ridiculous headgear that some players seem to feel is obligatory on those occasions. After a few glasses of champagne in the dressing room, it was back to Birmingham and another fantastic night at the Baggot Arms.

16/3/1977 (REPLAY) ASTON VILLA 1 EVERTON 1 (AET) HILLSBOROUGH

BURRIDGE, GIDMAN AND ROBSON; PHILLIPS, NICHOLL AND MORTIMER; DEEHAN,
LITTLE, GRAY, COWANS AND CARRODUS.

13/4/1977 (SECOND REPLAY) ASTON VILLA 3 EVERTON 2 (AET) OLD TRAFFORD
BURRIDGE, GIDMAN AND ROBSON; PHILLIPS, NICHOLL AND MORTIMER; GRAYDON,
LITTLE, DEEHAN, CROPLEY AND COWANS. SUB: SMITH.

At that time I was playing the best football of my career. I was part
of a very good side with a great bunch of lads, the fans seemed to
appreciate my efforts, and I was enjoying it immensely. I also felt that I
was playing well enough for a Scotland recall, but at that time Scotland
were blessed with loads of talented forwards such as Masson, Rioch,
Jordon, Hartford, Macari, Dalglish, Gemmill and Willie Johnstone,
who had all established themselves as regulars since my last game, and
it would have been extremely difficult to dislodge them from the side.
Every player wants to play for his country and I was no exception,
but although I still checked the newspapers, after missing so many
internationals over the past five years I now didn't really expect to be
selected and it didn't bother me all that much.

We defeated our great rivals West Bromwich Albion 4-0 at Villa
Park in the final game to bring the curtain down on what had been a
great season for the club. Andy Gray and Brian Little had formed a
particularly productive partnership scoring 55 goals between them in
all games as Villa finally finished in fourth place in the table, only six
points behind champions Liverpool who were winning the title for a
second consecutive season. It was the club's best league position since
finishing second in 1932–33, 44 years before. We had taken many
people by surprise and had still been in contention for the league title
until the closing weeks of the season, but perhaps the major drawback
had been the lack of depth in our squad, injuries to key players,
particularly near the end taking a heavy toll.

In the FA Cup we had come unstuck in the fourth round with a
2-1 home defeat by Manchester United after earlier victories against
Leicester City, West Ham and Port Vale. As a club however we were
then on the crest of a wave. These were great days and things could
only get better. Little did I know, or possibly I should have in the
circumstances, that trouble lay just around the corner.

CHAPTER ELEVEN

In Europe with the Villa
and a Clash with Ally Brown

AS A REWARD for winning the League Cup, at the end of the season all the players, management, coaching staff, wives and girlfriends were taken on a week-long all expenses paid holiday to Marbella in Spain. There were no games, just total relaxation in the sun; Gordon Smith relaxing more than most one evening and having to be carried from the taxi, losing his glasses in the process. These trips were great for team spirit and it was fun all the way. At our hotel there were numerous games, including one based loosely on volleyball in which the players, some of the wives and even several of the other hotel guests would join in. 'Budgie' as usual would take things over-seriously, often knocking women and young children out of the way to get to the ball.

We were surprised to see the then Southampton manager Lawrie McMenemy appear at the hotel one day, and it later turned out that he was there to sign Chris Nicholl. Unknown to us Saunders had already agreed the transfer of the Everton centre half Ken McNaught as Chris's replacement. Chris was now around 32 and although he had rarely let us down it was common knowledge that the manager really fancied McNaught who had played so well against us in the cup final. Ken, son of the famous Scottish international Willie McNaught of Raith Rovers, was a big gruff lad and it took him quite a while to settle in at Villa Park. At Goodison he had played alongside Mick Lyons, a player who was similar in style and I think that he needed time in adapting to playing alongside Leighton Phillips who was much more of a ball player. Ken was a bit on the quiet side, which is unusual for a 'Fifer', but he was a canny lad and became very popular with the rest of the players.

One afternoon near the end of the holiday Liz and I were having a massive row on the rocks at the end of the beach when who should pass by on a boat but chairman Sir William Dugdale, who shouted over: 'hello Mr and Mrs Cropley, how are you enjoying yourselves?' There is no way that he could have avoided hearing us shouting and screaming at each other at the top of our voices, and I wished that the ground could have opened up and swallowed us.

Unfortunately the arguments continued when we arrived back in Birmingham, and for whatever reason I decided to tell Liz that I had met someone else. For many months now she had not been coming down to Birmingham. We had still been living at the hotel and it was my idea that she and Jennifer should remain in Edinburgh, while I travelled back to see them most weekends.

Obviously with Liz back in Scotland I was spending a lot of time on my own. One night Gordon Smith and I were invited to take part in a sports forum at the supporters' club near the ground. Gordon knew some of the office staff who worked at Villa Park and at the end of the evening we started chatting over a few drinks. It was totally unplanned and so very innocent, but one thing led to another and although I knew it was wrong I started to see a girl called Pat Yeomans regularly. It turned out that Liz had her suspicions for some time that all was not well, but that obviously didn't prevent her from blowing her top and she left immediately for Edinburgh. To cut a long story short, we decided to separate, and I eventually moved in with Pat. Everything was totally my fault, and I'm sad to say that I didn't handle the situation very well. It had been common knowledge among the players and staff for some time that Pat and I were an item, even Ron Saunders on one occasion asking me if I was sure that I knew what I was doing, but unfortunately there was now no turning back.

Pat and I eventually moved into the house Liz and I were having built at Sutton Coldfield, but it took me a long time to finally get over the breakdown of the marriage.

Again I make no apology for going on about pre-season training, but I was surprised at just how many managers failed completely to understand the benefit of making training, particularly the exhausting pre-season work, as interesting as possible. The players can still be put through their paces, but if the exercises are varied and interesting it stands to reason that they will enjoy it that bit more and consequently should work that bit harder. Ron Saunders knew a farmer who allowed us the use of one of his fields for pre-season training. Measuring roughly two lengths of a football pitch, it had a slight incline and we would tackle this field in a figure of eight formation for hour after hour becoming more and more bored as the day wore on. If that wasn't bad enough, in midweek hurdles were introduced for us to manoeuvre, and Andy Gray, Frank Carrodus and Tommy Craig would blame the hard landing from the hurdles for the cartilage trouble that they later encountered.

Meanwhile Villa had been invited to take part in a four team pre-season tournament in Bilbao along with the host side Athletico, Dynamo Kiev and Anderlecht. I had taken a slight knock during training and was not considered for any of the games and watched from the bench. During the match against Bilbao, 'Budgie', who as I have said was a great shot stopper but a bit on the small side for a goalkeeper and not all that great in the air, failed to come out for a cross ball allowing our opponents to score. It was just the latest in a series of mistakes made by the goalkeeper. Burridge was a strong character and he and the manager did not get on particularly well. I think that Saunders had now had enough and during the game he asked my opinion of my former teammate Jimmy Rimmer, who at that time had lost his place at Arsenal to Pat Jennings. 'Budgie' was a friend of mine but I had to be honest and tell Saunders that I considered Rimmer to be an excellent goalkeeper, brave, good in the air and extremely reliable. I thought no more about it at the time but soon after arriving back in Birmingham I discovered that Rimmer had joined us from Arsenal. Unfortunately, that was the end at Villa Park for 'Budgie' who would soon be on his way to Southend on loan before a more permanent transfer to Crystal Palace. It was the start of an incredible journey for the goalkeeper that would eventually see him play for another 18 teams before finally hanging up his gloves.

Apart from Rimmer there were other additions to the squad around that time. John Gregory joined us from Northampton along with centre half Alan Evans from Dunfermline. While Gregory was an elegant player with a bit of pace, Evans in direct contrast was a rugged, and I do mean rugged, centre half who would kick his granny. After a fairly quiet start Alan would form a great defensive partnership with Ken McNaught, eventually going on to give the club 12 years of sterling service before a move to Leicester City late in his career. 'Budgies' replacement, Jimmy Rimmer, was a fantastic goalkeeper. Possibly because he had been relegated to the reserves at Arsenal, he was determined to do well at Villa Park and tried even harder than before. He was a fantastic trainer and I used to watch him going through his own routine when he would sprint around the pitch stopping at each junction for a punishing set of press ups. Unfortunately, Jimmy tried hard to be one of the lads but for some reason I never felt that he was on the same wavelength as the rest of us.

After our cup win everyone knew that the coming season was going to be much harder than ever. The Villa supporters were a demanding bunch and were now expecting a lot more of us. The previous season we had perhaps been something of an unknown quantity taking some teams by surprise, but the cup win had changed all that. Now they were well aware of just how good we could be, and often raised their game against us. We ourselves were not taking things any easier, but perhaps things that had come off for us during the previous season were not always going our way now.

The new season started well enough with a 2-1 victory over Queens Park Rangers in London, but only a week later we were murdered 4-1 by a very good Manchester City at Villa Park. Although the game was probably as good as lost at the time, in the second half I made certain when I sent a careless pass across my own 18 yard box that was intercepted by Dennis Tueart who took advantage of the gift to score. I accepted the deserved bollocking from the boss in the dressing room after the game without complaint.

The one thing we all really looked forward to were the European games. Whether it was Easter Road, Highbury or any other ground they were always great occasions, and at Villa Park the atmosphere on these special nights was absolutely fantastic. The aura of the floodlights as you approached the ground, the huge crowds and the added uncertainty of the sometimes unknown but often formidable opponents all added to the experience.

Just a few weeks after opening our defence of the League Cup with a 3-1 away victory over Exeter City, Andy Gray scoring a hat-trick, we faced the Turkish side Ferenbahce in the first round of the UEFA Cup at Villa Park. Our 4-0 win was achieved easily enough with goals from the forward trio of Dixie Deehan who scored two, Andy Gray and Brian Little, but to be fair to our opponents this was in the days before Turkish football was in the ascendancy. The return leg in Turkey however was something else. Istanbul itself was a beautiful city but at the stadium we took the field to face an unbelievably hostile crowd. The pitch was surrounded by a wide running track but this did little to prevent their fans from pelting us throughout with any missile that came to hand, apples, buns, toffee apples, you name it. They were a very poor side and we more than held our own, eventually running out deserved 2-0 winners. Throughout the 90 minutes the big Turkish striker had been proving a real handful, but our centre half Leighton Phillips was giving as good as he got. The next thing we knew there was blood everywhere after Leighton had been head butted by his opponent. For a while there was mayhem as the players of both sides jostled each other before things were eventually calmed down by the referee. As far as I'm aware the Ferenbahce player was not even booked, and after the extremely unwelcoming reception by the highly strung Turkish fans we were mightily relieved to hear the final whistle.

By then we were going fairly well in the league with only two defeats from our last seven games including a 1-0 victory at home against Arsenal. As I've said its always a great feeling putting one over on your former side and again this time was no exception. It had been a dour affair with few chances at either end although Arsenal had been much the better side. With the game looking every inch a stalemate, in the very last minute I swung a leg at a Carrodus cross that had been helped on by Andy Gray, and probably caught out my quick reactions, my shot from just outside the penalty area beat Pat Jennings at his far post. It turned out to be the only goal of the game against an Arsenal side who rightly felt aggrieved at the final result, and in the circumstances the victory gave me particular pleasure. Afterwards, Ron Saunders moaned that it had been our worst performance of the season so far, but I'm sure that wouldn't have bothered the delighted Villa fans.

The victory over Ferenbahce had paired us against the Polish side Gornik Zabrze, the first game again at Villa Park. Ken McNaught scored both our goals that night with typical centre half headers from corners as we cantered to a 2-0 win. They were his first goals for the club and he was particularly delighted that they had come in such an important game. It had taken Ken a while to settle in at the Villa but against Gornik he had been immense, and I think that this was possibly the turning point for him at the club.

An Andy Gray goal in the return leg in Poland was enough to give us a 1-1 draw and a 3-1 victory on aggregate, but in Zagreb it had been all hands to the pumps. They weren't a bad side and on a heavy pitch they tried to batter us from the start, but we played well ourselves and more than held our own. Up front Andy Gray's movement was different class, his intelligent runs causing all kinds of bother in the opposition penalty area. He had great support from both Brian Little who was playing a bit deeper off the centre half and John Deehan, until John was replaced late in the game by Gordon Cowans. Although I was still relatively quiet, unlike the dressing room jokers Andy Gray and John Gidman with whom there was never a dull moment, I was anything but quiet on the field. The fans had taken to my forceful style of play and it was always a great feeling to hear them singing my name. Andy Gray often told me that I flew into tackles, but in those days I think that most players did. I could also be a real moaner on the pitch. Brian Little could be a quiet lad and sometimes not the most energetic. Against Zabrze I was constantly complaining that he was not closing down their full backs. Not normally one to say boo to a goose, Brian eventually turned and gave me a mouthful back which stunned me, but I was delighted that at least I had got a reaction from him.

On these European trips I sometimes roomed with Andy Gray but after the game in Zagreb we were due to fly straight home. This was great news for Andy and Gordon Smith who had both been invited to a late night party in Birmingham. Unfortunately the heavy mist that had lingered over the stadium all evening later got decidedly worse and our flight had to be delayed until the next morning. On hearing the news Andy and Gordon went ballistic, cursing and shouting, the rest of us in stitches at their antics.

In between the games against Gornik we had drawn with West Ham, beaten Queens Park Rangers in the next round of the League Cup, and defeated Manchester United 2-1 at Villa Park when I managed to score only my second goal of the season. At that time United were a middle of the table side managed by Dave Sexton who had only recently taken over from Tommy Docherty, but with players of the calibre of Steve Coppell, Gordon Hill, Jimmy Greenhoff, my old sparring partner at Aberdeen Martin Buchan and Arthur Albiston who hailed from Edinburgh, they were never going to be an easy side to beat and we considered it a decent enough victory.

Seven days after the Manchester United game we had another great result when we defeated Liverpool 2-0, and at Anfield at that, Andy Gray scoring both our goals. That afternoon we didn't half play well, denying Liverpool the ball. Everything just clicked and the victory was all the sweeter as they were the reigning champions.

In the third round of the UEFA Cup we were drawn against our summer hosts Athetico Bilbao at Villa Park. There was no scoring when midway through the first half goalkeeper Irabar dropped the ball over the line from one of my corners to give us the lead. I discovered later that it had been put down to an own goal, denying me only my third strike of the season so far. John Deehan scored the other as we eventually ran out fairly easy 2-0 winners.

Our hold on the League Cup was finally relinquished when we went down 4-2 to Brian Clough's Nottingham Forest at the City Ground in the third round. This was followed by yet another defeat at Ipswich. I had picked up a slight injury against Forest and missed the game at Portman Road and also the return leg of the UEFA Cup against Bilbao, but was fit in time for the big Birmingham derby against West Bromwich Albion at Villa Park. If you ask any old military man his service number, even years later he will be able to reel it off instantly. For me the date: 10 December 1977, at 3.46pm; will be imprinted on my brain forever. That was the day and exact time that I suffered the fourth, and worst by far, leg break of my career.

I remember that it was a typical cold winter's day. There was no wind and the pitch was fairly wet. The games against West Brom were always tousy affairs capable of attracting a huge crowd, and this one was no different. It was a typical derby played in a cup tie atmosphere and with the score still at nothing each, near the end of the first half Chris Nicholl was carried off and replaced by our substitute Gordon Cowans. Just a few minutes later I went into a tackle with Albion's Scottish midfielder Ally Brown. I just managed to nick the ball away from Brown when with all my weight on my left leg he took me, ball, the lot, sending me flying through the air. There is no mistaking the crack from a broken leg. The sound reverberates throughout your body and I immediately feared the worst. Although there was no pain I was lying on the ground going absolutely ballistic, screaming and swearing that he had done me. I was immediately surrounded by a ruck of concerned players but can still remember looking through a gap in their legs to see that Andy Gray had Brown by the neck over the enclosure wall, and still in my confused state, I wondered why he was doing it. At that time Villa had a lovely old odd job man we called 'Pop' who had served with the army during the Great War. I remember 'Pop' coming on to the field to offer me a drink of brandy which I refused. At that he promptly drank the brandy himself.

I was rushed by stretcher to Good Hope Hospital where I was to be operated on immediately, and I arrived at the hospital to see Doctor Cheyne, who was to perform the operation already waiting for me still dressed in his gardening gear after being called unexpectedly from home.

I awoke from the anaesthetic a short while later to find Pat at my bedside. She had been at the game with her dad and told me that the crack of my leg breaking could clearly be heard even above the roars of the 40-odd thousand spectators who were packed inside the ground. Later that evening I received a visit from the Aston Villa director Doug Ellis who came out of his way to see me at the hospital. Before leaving Doug wanted to know if I needed anything. Because I hadn't yet spoken to my mum or dad I asked if he had any loose change for the phone at which he promptly thrust a five pound note into my hand! A colourful and controversial figure who had made his fortune selling package holidays to Spain, Ellis had been chairman of the club since 1968 until replaced by Sir William Dugdale in 1975. As chairman he had been instrumental in the signing of Ron Saunders as manager although it was now well known that the two disliked each other intensely. Nicknamed 'Deadly Doug' by the former England player Jimmy Greaves because of his penchant for sacking managers, Ellis was never overly popular with the Aston Villa supporters who accused him of lacking ambition for the club, but regardless I really appreciated his visit.

I was to receive another surprise visitor that evening in the shape of Ron Saunders who only stayed long enough to collect my jersey. I was still fairly groggy from the anaesthetic and feeling a bit sorry for myself and in the circumstances I was extremely disappointed at the sole reason behind his visit.

That night I watched the game on TV to see a Villa side that had played entire second half with ten men eventually win 3-0 with goals scored by Cowans, Gray and Gidman, and it was quite surreal to see the lead up to the leg break. I had known Ally Brown since our school days in Scotland and to my mind he was a decent, skilful player, not one that would deliberately set out to harm anyone and I would like to think that the tackle had merely been mistimed. West Brom themselves couldn't have been better, sending me in a gigantic bouquet of flowers and a bottle of champagne accompanied by a letter of condolence. The gesture was greatly appreciated, although perhaps I was a bit disappointed that Ally Brown himself didn't visit me in hospital. I was also inundated with literally hundreds of cards from well-wishers from all over the country including one from both Arsenal and Hibs, all wishing me a speedy recovery, and I was totally knocked out at their genuine concern.

I was in hospital for only three days but the injury seemed to take forever to heal, well over six months and certainly much longer than any of the others. At times I was driven to near despair with boredom. Sitting in the house all day reading books was not for me and I must have watched every cowboy film that was ever made on TV. Although it had been a clean break, both the Tibia and Fibula had gone. For a while there was a real concern about the supply of blood to the area and at one stage a bone graft was considered, something that didn't exactly fill me with confidence. I would visit Doctor Cheyne at the hospital every few weeks but months later the injury still didn't appear to be healing. One day Pat's mother suggested that I should try the faith healer who had recently cured the long standing pain in her back. I wasn't convinced, but at that stage I was willing to try anything. At his home the healer took my left knee in one hand and started to massage the area above the injury through the plaster with the other. This went on for some time and I could feel the strangest sensation of warmth around the area. I had some reservations about telling Doctor Cheyne about the faith healer when I next visited the hospital, but he didn't seem to mind, saying that if I felt I was getting better then it wouldn't do me any harm. Whether it had been due to the faith healer or not I will never know, but suffice to say, when Doctor Cheyne removed the plaster the injury seemed to have healed naturally, and now thankfully there would be no need for another operation.

And so the long slog to full fitness began all over again. After the final removal of the much lighter plaster I had to learn to walk again before gentle runs around the streets near the stadium wearing heavy hiking boots, gradually increasing in tempo and distance. There were also exercises like kicking a medicine ball with my injured leg, either that or our fitness coach would lie on the ground with a medicine ball at arm's length for me to strike. Either way I found it a really hard slog and I would not play again that season. I had also learned to be more patient regarding my recovery. Before, I would have been champing at the bit to get back; but experience had taught me that I would be back only when I was ready. The hardest part had been when my leg was encased in the extremely restrictive full plaster, but it was only once that was removed almost six months to the day from the injury that I started to improve step by step.

While I was still recuperating I decided to visit my former teammate at Hibs, John Blackley, who was then with Newcastle United at his hotel before a game against the West Brom at the Hawthorns. Unknown to me the Albion players were also having their pre-match meal at the same hotel and I accidentally bumped into Ally Brown. He was about to greet me warmly when he saw the plaster sticking out from below my trousers and couldn't get away fast enough, which I suppose was fair enough considering the circumstances.

A fall in the house during the Christmas period threatened to delay my recovery but fortunately a hospital check-up later revealed no serious damage to the injured leg. It wasn't all plain sailing though, and a newspaper reporter happened to catch me on a bad day when I was really down when I confessed that after so many bad injuries I was seriously thinking about calling it a day. It was a consideration however that never really crossed my mind. I loved the game and just wanted to play.

Meanwhile Villa had drawn Everton at Goodison in the first round of the FA Cup. Unable to make the journey to Liverpool I was invited to watch the game live on the television monitors at the ATV studios in Birmingham which I thought was a lovely gesture. Unfortunately any thoughts of FA Cup glory for Villa were put on hold for at least another year when Everton scored four against a consolation from Andy Gray.

After many months of hard work I eventually regained something resembling full fitness although I never did regain 100% mobility of the knee after arthritis had set in.

Around about then Andy Gray, Frank Carrodus and myself all found ourselves recovering from injury at the same time. The club sent all three of us for a week's intensive treatment at a clinic at Bowden, staying at the local hotel. At the hotel we would order huge steaks, all the trimmings and the best of wine, but there was hell to pay a few weeks later when Aston Villa received the bill and we were all called into the manager's office. Fortunately we escaped punishment by explaining that we felt it was only right that we should treat the staff at the clinic after their tremendous care and attention to our injuries, which of course was complete rubbish.

Although I was still incapacitated at the time I was really enjoying being part of such a great club. I had settled in well to life in Birmingham. When I had visited the city before as an Arsenal player I had travelled by team coach and didn't really know where Birmingham was, now I was totally settled in the place, was accepted by the players and fans, and felt as though I had lived in the city for years.

CHAPTER TWELVE

A Brief Return to Action

WHILE THE REST of the villa players were lounging about on foreign beaches during the summer it was business as usual for me as I continued my build up to full fitness with daily exercises and runs around the streets of Birmingham. Later I managed to complete the tough pre-season training with the rest of the lads although I was still some way behind, but I was champing at the bit to get back playing. I was still under the orders of Doctor Cheyne who considered that I was not yet quite ready to return, and in any case I was obviously well short of match practice. My parents had come down from Edinburgh on holiday and Dad would occasionally come and watch the pre-season training at Bodymoor Heath. One morning on the way back to the house he said to me: 'there will be a few players looking over their backs when you come back', a remark that completely stunned me. It was one of the very few times that I can ever remember him giving me praise.

I would go along to watch as many of the first team games as I could, including a League Cup tie against Crystal Palace when 'Budgie' was on top form against his former teammates, but watching from the side-lines only increased my craving to get back playing again.

At last I received the news I had been waiting weeks to hear when the doctor gave me the all clear, and on 28 October I made my return to action when I managed to play the full 90 minutes against Sheffield United reserves at Bramall Lane in a Central League game. We lost 3-1 but the score was the last thing on my mind. I was determined to put in a hard tackle early on and was delighted when I felt no reaction from the injury. I was absolutely shattered at the end but it was just great to be back, and I came on for the last 20 minutes in the John

Robson Testimonial game at Villa Park a couple of days later.

Unfortunately by then John had been diagnosed as suffering from the serious debilitating illness, Multiple Sclerosis, that was eventually to cost him his life, and had been forced to give up the game. On the night of the testimonial the fans enjoyed a fantastic evening of football as Aston Villa and an International XI served up a feast of entertainment, sharing 12 goals. Many of the top players in the game gave up their time for such a worthy cause and we were all delighted that over £30,000 was raised for John. Ron Saunders had promised that I would get on at some stage but as the proceedings wore on I was getting more and more restless. Kenny Dalglish on the opposition bench could see this and started winding me up by shouting across: 'Put him on, Ron, put him on', which seemed to make Saunders all the more dogmatic and me more and more frustrated. Eventually I was told to get changed and to hear the crowd chanting my name as I stripped was music to my ears. I can't remember my first touch but I certainly can my second when I scored what the press later described as a wonder goal when I smashed a first time volley past Ray Clemence and into the roof of the net from 25 yards. I don't know if it was a wonder goal, but it certainly did wonders for my confidence.

ASTON VILLA: RIMMER, GIDMAN AND WILLIAMS; EVANS, MCNAUGHT AND GREGORY; CRAIG, LITTLE, GRAY, DEEHAN AND SHELTON. SUBS: CROPLEY AND PHILLIPS.

INTERNATIONAL XI: CLEMENCE (LIVERPOOL), CALDERWOOD (BIRMINGHAM) AND SANSOM (ARSENAL); MCKENZIE (CHELSEA), NICHOLL (SOUTHAMPTON) AND BUCHAN (MANCHESTER UNITED); MACARI (MANCHESTER UNITED), BROOKING (WEST HAM), DALGLISH (LIVERPOOL), VILLA (TOTTENHAM HOTSPUR) AND HILL (DERBY COUNTY). SUBS: GILLARD (QUEENS PARK RANGERS), BUCKLEY (BIRMINGHAM), WALLACE (COVENTRY CITY) AND HUTCHISON (COVENTRY CITY).

After the goal I could hear the fans chanting 'Cropley is back, Cropley is back', which was music to my ears, but unfortunately it was not to be quite as simple as that. Although I had been cleared to play by Doctor Cheyne, for some reason Ron Saunders was reluctant to give me a first team start and I spent the next few weeks in the reserves champing at the bit, until finally, almost a year to the day since breaking my leg against West Brom, I was named as a substitute against Chelsea at the Bridge. Although Villa collected both points after Alan Evans scored the only goal of the game, for me the result was secondary and I was delighted to make my comeback when I replaced Gary Shaw with just eight minutes remaining. It was not long enough to make any kind of impact and although it was great to be back to where I thought I should be, it was still not all plain sailing. Over the next couple of months there would be only sporadic appearances in the first team, sometimes as a substitute, and it was not until a 4-0 defeat away to Nottingham Forest at the beginning of April that I finally felt I had recaptured my rightful place in the side.

A 3-1 home win against Liverpool was followed by a fine 2-1 away win against Norwich during which I managed to score my first goal of the season. There was another great 5-1 win against my former side Arsenal, although I have to say that a few weeks later we were murdered 3-0 at Anfield when Liverpool gained sweet revenge for the earlier defeat at Villa Park. Liverpool's Terry McDermott was renowned for his forward runs and that afternoon I was slaughtered big time as he ran rings round me. I was furious to be taken off and replaced by Ivor Linton, as with all due respect to Ivor I knew that I was a better player than him, but looking back the manager was probably right as I had been getting the run around all afternoon.

Since the game against Forest I had kept my place in the side for all 12 of the remaining fixtures and had the satisfaction of scoring Villa's final goal of the season in a fine 3-2 win at Maine Road.

A season that had mostly been a complete waste of time, as far as I was concerned anyway, ended with Aston Villa in eighth place in the table, four places worse off than the previous season and a colossal 22 points behind champions Liverpool. As well as 14 appearances for the reserves I had managed just 17 first team appearances including four as substitute, scoring two goals, but it was just great to be back.

CHAPTER THIRTEEN

Newcastle, Toronto
and a Nightmare at Portsmouth

THE 1979–80 SEASON would be a momentous one for me, my last as it would turn out as a first division footballer.

It had all started well enough. After the trials and tribulations of the previous 18 months I was now really fit, or as fit as a player who has suffered two cartilage operations, a broken ankle and three broken legs, could reasonably expect to be, and I was raring to go.

At Villa Park the personnel had changed considerably since the previous season. Andy Gray had moved on and would soon be followed out the door by John Gidman. Both had been in dispute with the club for some time. I never really found out the real reason but could only guess that Ron Saunders had a lot to do with it as it was well known that they didn't get on with each other. Things had been okay at the beginning but some of the players were now questioning Ron Saunders tactical ability and the pair had become disillusioned. Gray had moved to Wolves the previous season for a then British record fee of £1.5 million pounds and he would win the League Cup by scoring the winner against Nottingham Forest in the coming season. After a few games Gidman would leave to join Everton and was replaced by my former teammate at Hibs Des Bremner. Des was similar in style to John, and what a good signing he turned out to be. He had improved out of all recognition since making his debut for Hibs in 1973 and it had cost Villa the best part of £270,000 to secure his services with the former Clyde player Joe Ward going in the opposite direction as a £70,000 makeweight in the deal. The full back pairing was now between Kenny Swain the former Chelsea forward, and Colin Gibson who had come through the ranks at Villa Park. The former Stoke City defender Mike Pejik had been signed from Everton but unfortunately Mike's time at Aston Villa would be cut short due to injury and he would retire after only around a dozen games. Gary Shaw had also come through the ranks and was now ready to claim a regular first team place. Tommy Craig had been signed from Newcastle United in 1978, but had not really settled at Villa Park, possibly due to injury, and he had moved on to Swansea during the previous season.

After a 1-1 draw with Bolton Wanderers at Burnden Park on the opening day of the new season we faced newly promoted Brighton at Villa Park. After only 14 minutes I was involved in an innocuous tackle with Brighton's Brian Horton. I can honestly say that it was the only time I can remember going into a tackle completely the wrong way. Usually I went in strong with all my weight behind me but this time I went in weakly with the side of the foot, resulting in my left ankle being turned. It was instantly obvious that I was unable to continue and I was helped from the field by trainer Roy McLaren to be replaced by Lee Jenkins, one of only three games that Lee would play for Villa, all as a substitute, before a move to Port Vale. Once again I didn't think the injury was all that serious at the time but an X-ray later revealed that I had cracked a bone in my ankle and once again it was off to see Doctor Cheyne at Good Hope hospital. Once again a restrictive plaster was considered, but because arthritis had set in from the previous injuries, it was decided to insert a screw into the bone instead. This would allow me more mobility and enable me to get about with only the aid of walking sticks, which was great news for me. Financially things were okay as I was still part of the first team pool, but little did I know it at the time that I had played my last game for the first team.

Once again it was a long road to recovery lasting several months. In those situations it's so important that you don't despair. It's so easy to let your head go down and its vital that you keep your spirits up which luckily for me was now part of my make-up and I made my return in a reserve game around December. I was still on first team bonuses so there was no problem there, but ask any player who is accustomed to playing first team football and he will tell you that playing in the reserves for any length of time is simply soul destroying.

Just before a game against Manchester City reserves at Villa Park I had been approached in the foyer by the then Celtic manager Billy McNeill and coach John Clark who enquired about my injured leg.

They then stunned me by asking if I would be interested in returning to Scotland to play with Celtic. Although Celtic had won the league in Scotland the previous season I had to be honest and say that at that particular time I still felt that I had a future at Aston Villa. I had one of my better games that afternoon but by the end of the game both McNeill and Clark had left and no more was heard about a move to Celtic. I disliked playing in the reserves but to give him his due Bill Shorthouse, the Villa trainer, would do his best to keep my spirits up by urging me to work harder as I was not far away. I was virtually ignored by the manager however who perhaps understandably was more concerned with the first team players, and I now knew that no matter how well I played for the reserves or how many goals I scored, that there would be little chance of a quick recall to the league side.

One day Saunders took me aside to ask if I would consider going out on loan. The idea interested me although I didn't just want to go anywhere, but when I heard that it was Newcastle United, then top of the Second Division, who were interested I jumped at the chance. Apparently the Newcastle manager Bill McGarry wanted me on a month's loan to prove myself before a possible permanent move. McGarry is reported as saying:

I have been searching for a replacement for long term casualty Mick Martin. The twice capped Scotland star Cropley is well equipped to fit the bill and I have been chasing the lad for two months. Only first team football will give him the chance to get his confidence back and I'm offering him the opportunity to prove he still has what it takes.

By now Pat and I had a son, Ross, who had been born at Good Hope hospital in Birmingham in 1978, not long after my encounter with Ally Brown, and after talking it over with Pat, all three of us travelled up to Newcastle where we were put up in a hotel for the month. I trained that morning with my new teammates before watching from the stand as they went down 5-1 to Leicester City in the afternoon, and made my debut on the Wednesday when we got another right good going over from Wrexham when we were lucky only to lose 3-1. This was followed by a drab, dour and depressing 0-0 draw against Birmingham City. A free Saturday saw us travelling up to Scotland to play Dundee in a friendly. I thought I was doing reasonably well but in Kenny Hibbitt Newcastle had another player who was all left sided and possibly we were too similar in style to be effective. There was yet another defeat, this time by Shrewsbury during which I was subbed at half time. While possibly not the best player on the park I was certainly not the worst, and its fair to say that I was not overly pleased at getting taken off. A reporter called me at home on the Sunday asking for my views on the game, and somewhat rashly I told him that even Pele couldn't play in this team. That was the end for me at Newcastle. Understandably my comments didn't go down too well with McGarry and I was called into his office on the Monday morning where we both decided that it would perhaps be best if we called it a day, and it was back to the Villa reserves for me.

At that time Newcastle had some very good players including Peter Withe and John Brownlie. Peter was the top man at St James' Park and he took everything, and I mean everything – centres, corners, free kicks, penalties, throw-ins, you name it, the lot. The former Everton player Jim Pearson was also at St James' Park at that time, but diplomatically I never mentioned the League Cup final. Stewart Boam who had accidentally broken my leg when Arsenal played Middlesbrough all those months before was now at United. Stewart was a really good lad, and he couldn't believe all that I had gone through when I reminded him of the incident. My old teammate at Hibs John Brownlie was one of the mainstays of the side and it was great to catch up with him again, but in all honesty I couldn't get away from the place fast enough. For such a prominent side the training facilities were second rate, and while the trainer Ian McFaul was a nice man, in my opinion he was not all that good at the job. The main reason I left however was Bill McGarry. McGarry was another whom I considered tactically inept, and I didn't have much time for him. To my mind he was in exactly the same mould as Ron Saunders, dour, lacking even the remotest hint of man management, and as far as I could see was not overly popular with the rest of the players.

I was not long back in the Villa reserves when the former Bolton player Ian Greaves, then manager of Oxford, offered me another loan deal. At our meeting things seemed to go well, so I was not particularly happy to read in the papers that the deal was off. Surprised as well as disappointed that I had found out only through the media, I phoned Ian to say thanks for nothing.

Derby County were the next to show an interest, but in their case it was a permanent move. I met manager Colin Addison at a hotel in Birmingham and again things appeared to have gone well, so it was a major blow when I was informed by Ron Saunders a few days later that I had failed the medical. With my track record of injuries the verdict was perhaps foreseeable, but it was a real blow as I had really looked forward to signing for another first division club, although they would be relegated at the end of the season.

Pat and I next travelled down to Watford to meet manager Graeme Taylor in a car borrowed from Andy Gray. It was a real flying machine but unfortunately there was no water in it and on the way back it blew up and we just managed to limp home. Andy being Andy just shrugged his shoulders at the news. Although I didn't think that I had been asking Watford for the moon, Graeme soon phoned to inform me that the deal had fallen through because they couldn't afford to pay me what I was asking. Although I understood completely, once again I was extremely disappointed as I had liked the manager and had been impressed at the set-up.

I was still playing for the reserves, but a few weeks later I was again called into Ron Saunders office, this time to be told me that he couldn't keep playing me as I was preventing some of the promising youngsters from breaking through. I could well understand the manager's position, and with no need to keep training, Pat and I spent the rest of the season back in Edinburgh.

One day while walking along Princes Street I happened to bump into the Hibs chairman Tom Hart who invited me to a game at Easter Road. That Saturday my friend Mike Collins and I were sitting in the Directors Box watching the game. Football fans being what they are it was not long before the rumours started flying around that I was re-signing for the club. The supporters however were beside themselves trying to put a name to the mystery player sitting beside me. Mike and I later had a good laugh about it.

While I was in Edinburgh Ron Saunders phoned me to say that although I still had a year of my three-year contract to run he would release me if I could find another club. By then I knew fine well that there was no way back for me at Aston Villa and the news was okay by me. It did however leave me in a quandary. I had been in the game for more than ten years, knew little else, and was now uncertain as to where my future now lay.

I had heard a lot about the North American Soccer League and quite fancied a stint over there. At that time I was quite friendly with Bruce Rioch who at one time had trained with us at Villa. I knew Bruce had played in America and phoned him to ask his advice. A move to Jacksonville was discussed but it turned out that they already had their allotted complement of players. With Bruce's help I was eventually put in touch with the Toronto Blizzard manager, Keith Eddy, who I had actually played against when he was with Sheffield United, and it was eventually agreed that I could join them for the rest of the summer season.

I phoned Ron Saunders to let him know the news and asked if I could keep the club car for services rendered. This seemed to create a major problem. Eventually after some haggling he agreed, but even then only if the deal was taxable.

Just before flying to Canada I received a phone call from the Portsmouth chairman John Deacon who was interested in signing me. I informed him that I had already signed for Toronto Blizzard but he and manager Frank Burrows still insisted in travelling up to Birmingham to see me and we met in a hotel in West Bromwich. Deacon was the Mayor of Southampton at the time and I thought that he was a bit of a chancer. He was keen for me to join Portsmouth on my return to Britain at the end of the North American season, and to make sure, despite it being highly illegal to sign for two clubs at the same time, I was handed a contract which I duly signed in pencil and it was kept in a drawer until my return from Canada.

The very next day Pat, Ross and I caught the flight to Toronto at the beginning of a brand new adventure. Toronto is a beautiful city, particularly at that time of the year, and the weather was fantastic. After a short stay in a hotel we were put up in a condominium, each flat with its own swimming pool. Among our near neighbours were the former West Ham and Bermuda player Clyde Best and Malcolm Robertson who hailed from Edinburgh. Malcolm had played for Hearts just after my time at Easter Road and would play a few games for Hibs a couple of years later. I never did find out what he did in his spare time, but we rarely saw Clyde outside of the football, although he would drive me to the games and training. Blizzard were far from the best team in the league but their set-up was impressive, the games taking place in the huge Varsity stadium which was also used for American football. They also had some very good players including Tor Cervin who had played for Malmo against Nottingham Forest in the European Cup final in Munich a couple of years before, and Jose Velasquez who had played such a prominent part in Scotland's 3-1 defeat by Peru during our ill-fated World Cup finals in Argentina in 1978. Defender Luigi Martini was a suave Italian who was also a licensed pilot. He once explained to us just how many seconds were the most dangerous times during take-off and landing, and during our many trips away we could all be heard counting the seconds down during either manoeuvre. The Varsity stadium was normally used by the American football side and the dressing rooms were absolutely enormous in order to accommodate the huge number of players in each team, each player allocated his own individual changing cubicle isolated from the others. I changed near to the former Manchester United player Jimmy Greenhoff and we soon became great friends. The general quality of play was quite poor, and compared to some of the others Jimmy and I were like Pele, although some of the sides featured players of the calibre of Johan Cruyff, Johan Neeskens and the future Celtic manager Wilhelm Jansen, but nevertheless I found the whole thing to be a most enjoyable experience. The only down side was the travelling. With the distances between the games often so great, travel to many of the away games involved flying, and if you also had a midweek game then you might well be away from home for most of the week. The average attendances for many of the games was also very poor, ours ranging around the 3,000 mark, although some of the better sides like New York and Chicago had a much larger fan base.

I had only been in Toronto a matter of weeks when I received a phone call from Andy Gray. With the English season now over Andy and his partner were holidaying in Florida and wanted to come up and visit us. What was initially meant to be a two week stay turned into a month and he would eventually train and play five a sides with us. Andy was well known in Canada and both the players and fans loved him. As I say the lifestyle was fabulous and, away from football, most of the day would be spent lounging around the pool. I had a pair of blue speedo swimming trunks when I arrived and at the end of our stay the sun had almost bleached them white.

One of our games entailed travelling down to play Chicago Stings at the famous Wrigley Field and I was looking forward to meeting up again with the former Hibs player Derek Spalding who was then playing for the Stings. Derek had married an American girl and had settled in the States after leaving Edinburgh. He would spend five seasons with a very good Chicago side before ironically ending his playing career with Toronto Blizzard.

At that time the Americans were beginning to take a greater interest in soccer as they called it, and the game was beamed live both in the states and back in Canada. We had a Scottish player in our side who hailed from Alloa but later took Canadian citizenship, called Graham Hartley. Graham was a good looking somewhat cocky lad who really thought he was the business. During the first half against the Stings, we were losing 1-0, when I gave the ball away 20 yards from our goal when my pass was intercepted. I immediately tackled the player but gave away a free kick. All of a sudden this Hartley started to scream and shout at me. As we lined up for the defensive wall Hartley continued to moan and in a moment of madness I head-butted him. Down he went with blood everywhere. Immediately realising the seriousness of the situation I tried to apologise but understandably he was having none of it. Our captain Bruce Wilson ran over to tell me that Hartley hadn't been moaning at me at all, but at the referee who had been standing behind me, for awarding the free kick. I was called over by the official who immediately ordered me off, but before I could move, one of my teammates informed the referee that he couldn't send me off for hitting one of my own teammates, which of course was total rubbish. A now clearly confused official, who I believe was from Ireland and very inexperienced, agreed, and I was let off with a final warning. By now I had clearly lost it, and within minutes a player fell to the ground after tackling me and I deliberately stood on his back. That was enough for the referee who ran across shouting 'I've got you now, I've got you now', and this time I *was* sent off. I was about to leave the field but saw that the home crowd were in an uncompromising mood and I decided that it would be far safer watching the rest of the game from the dugout. On arriving back in Toronto Malcolm Robertson advised me to stay on the plane for a while after the others had left, explaining that Hartley had a couple of brothers who were fairly wild characters and the chances were that they would be waiting for me. Luckily when I did eventually leave there was no one waiting at the terminal and I made it home safely. As expected I was called into the chairman's office on the Monday to be told that I was being fined two weeks wages which was fair enough. Outside the office who did I bump into but Hartley? I again attempted to apologise saying that I had been totally out of order and was prepared to return to Britain if that's what he wanted, but I was totally taken aback when Graham explained that I had done him a great favour. His nose had been broken previously and the latest incident had straightened it. He was delighted – all he had been worried about was his good looks.

At the end of the season I was invited to stay for the winter indoor league which I seriously considered but in the end we decided to come back home. By that time the English season was already underway but I told Frank Burrows that I was going to have two weeks holiday before coming down to the south coast. There was a surprise waiting for me however when I did eventually arrive at Portsmouth when Burrows informed me that the chairman was now refusing to pay me the terms we had earlier agreed, indeed it was a lot less. I was now in a quandary. Had there been anyone else on the scene then I definitely would not have accepted the reduced terms, but at that time none of the other clubs were aware that I was a free agent and my options were extremely limited. With no other option I reluctantly accepted the terms offered by Burrows.

The arrival of chairman John Deacon in 1972 had failed to improve things at second division Portsmouth and they were relegated that same season. As well as chairman of Portsmouth, Deacon was also Mayor of Southampton, which I thought was a bit strange as the two towns were great rivals. Staving off the threat of bankruptcy in 1976 Portsmouth had been forced to appoint a relatively inexperienced manager in the former Motherwell, Liverpool and Scotland player Ian St John who unfortunately could not save them from a further drop into the fourth division and he was replaced by the legendary former Portsmouth and England player Jimmy Dickinson. Frank Burrows had started his playing career in Scotland with Raith Rovers before moving south to play with mainly lower league sides in England. He had joined Portsmouth as Assistant manager to Dickinson in 1979, taking over the Fratton Park hot seat on the latter's resignation, leading the club to promotion from the Fourth Division in his first season.

At the medical I remember the doctor bursting into the cubicle to tell me that 'I was a wreck', something that I was obviously already well aware off. While in Toronto the team doctor, who by coincidence was a friend of Doctor McQuillan who had operated on me when I was with Hibs, had told me that he had seen it all now. 'Your knees are shot up, and with your style of play you should not really be doing this.'

Manager Frank Burrows was a really nice man, as honest as the day is long, but as far as football was concerned he lacked a lot and he would soon be replaced by my former coach at Arsenal, Bobby Campbell. On the day of what was to be my first game for the side, Burrows took me aside to tell me, for what reason I don't know, that I would not be playing after all, which really knocked me back, and even before kicking a ball I was already regretting signing for the club.

After playing in top class football for over ten years I found the third division a real struggle. Before I had been used to seeing plenty of the ball, but now for whatever reason, jealousy, or lack of talent, I felt that the ball was being deliberately kept away from me and I was not enjoying the game as before. There were lots of cliques in the dressing room and I didn't get on with most of the players who perhaps resented what they thought was a 'Billy Big Boots' from the first division, a fact probably not helped by me arriving at the ground every day driving the plush club car I had negotiated from Aston Villa. Also, as perhaps I should have expected from a lower league side, the training facilities were extremely poor and far different from what I had been used to. There was no actual training ground or gym, and we often utilised five different locations in the same week including a vacant area near the docks.

I had made less than a dozen appearances for Portsmouth when in one game I went in high to control the ball before my opponent could reach it. Unfortunately my foot caught his chest bending the knee back. In normal circumstances this wouldn't have been a problem, but with the reduced mobility in the leg due to my previous injuries, the knee bent back more than it could take and I immediately knew I was in trouble. After treatment it was obvious that I couldn't continue and although I was not to know it at that precise moment, after 14 years I had played my last ever game as a professional football player.

Unable to even take part in light training, I was sitting in the house a few weeks later when a letter from the Portsmouth lawyers popped through the letter box. The letter informed me bluntly that despite having signed a three-year contract that stipulated a 7% rise in wages each year, under employment law the football club were dispensing with my services with compensation amounting to just eight weeks wages.

With no other way at that time of earning a living I was forced to take the case to the Professional Footballers Association Union and I have to say that secretary Gordon Taylor did a first class job in presenting my case. At the hearing Taylor told the panel that as I still had a legal contract, it was binding, and had to be honoured. At that Deacon lost the plot screaming at Taylor – 'okay, tell Mr Cropley to be at Fratton Park on Monday morning for training'. Regardless of the fact that it was the close season I trained on my own for a few days until reason eventually prevailed and both parties accepted a compromise. Now I was to receive three months wages in full with a testimonial thrown in, which in the circumstances I suppose was fair enough.

The testimonial was arranged for the start of the following season with Aston Villa kindly agreeing to supply a strong side as the opposition. As promised Villa sent the complete European Cup winning side, and also the cup itself which was paraded around the ground before the start, but unfortunately the testimonial failed to prove as lucrative as it might have. At that time the Falklands war had just ended, and as well as a couple of pre-season friendly's against Ipswich and Liverpool, Portsmouth had also played a game to raise funds for the dependants of those killed on HMS Coventry which had been sunk during the campaign. All the games were played inside the space of a few days and perhaps understandably there was a very poor crowd inside Fratton Park for the game against Villa. By the time expenses for the police, programmes and the various other costs had been deducted there was little left. The biggest disappointment of the evening, however, had been the fact that I had not been fit enough to take part in the game itself.

Afterwards I obviously thanked the players of both sides for taking part in the game but I now regret that I didn't thank the crowd inside Fratton Park that did turn up. In the players' lounge after the game an old man thrust a ten pound note into my hand with the words: 'thanks – you were a player', words at that particularly low point in my life that were appreciated far more than he could ever know. One thing that did stick in my throat however was that I was expected to give the Portsmouth chairman John Deacon a momento as an acknowledgment for allowing the game to go ahead. I gave him a boxed pen set which he received without a word, and I have never been back to Portsmouth since.

CHAPTER FOURTEEN

A Sodjer's Return, Retirement
and the Story So Far

WITH MY CAREER as a professional football player now well and truly over, once again with the help of the PFA I applied to redeem the insurance policy that all professional players were obliged to take out. It proved to be an unbelievably complicated procedure but eventually with the invaluable help of Gordon Taylor, who once again was absolutely brilliant, the policy was settled in full and I now had to contemplate a future outside the game. The big problem however was what was I going to do now. The answer would come from an unexpected source.

After a managerial apprenticeship that included a spell as assistant to manager Alex Ferguson at Aberdeen, my former Hibs teammate Pat Stanton had only recently been appointed manager of the club. I was back in Edinburgh for a few days and decided to go and see Pat's first game in charge, a league fixture against St Mirren at Easter Road. It turned out to be a pretty dour and uninspiring no score draw, and after the game I was having a couple of beers in the private supporters' club across the road from the stadium when someone suggested that maybe I should go and see Stanton with a possible view to rejoining the club. This I eventually did, and during the meeting Pat asked if I thought I could do any better than the players he already had at his disposal. My answer: 'with one leg' seemed to confirm matters and after a quick meeting with chairman Kenny Waugh I was offered training facilities to see how things went. At that time the club was in a poor way. Relegated for only the second time in its history in 1980 they had been promoted again the following year, but it saddened me to see just how much the club had deteriorated in the space of only a few years. Only

175

Jim McArthur, Erich Schaedler and Arthur Duncan remained from my first spell at the club, although they were now approaching the veteran stage. Jimmy O'Rourke was now on the coaching staff with the evergreen Tom McNiven still working his miracles. After spells with Hearts and Newcastle, Ralph Callaghan, who in his younger days had been a regular in our Sunday morning games at Portobello, was now at Easter Road but even his undoubted talents could do little to lift the air of gloom that permeated throughout the club.

For several weeks I would spend all week training in Edinburgh only going home at the weekends, and eventually I was fit enough to be selected for the reserve side in a game against Dundee United reserves at Tannadice. We lost 4-0 and I found the going unbelievably tough but realised that it would take time to again achieve full match fitness. I took part in several other games including a fixture against Celtic reserves at Parkhead, but things finally came to a head in a game against Rangers second team when a Hibs side packed with inexperienced youngsters lost 6-0 at home. During the game the Hibs secretary Cecil Graham actually strode onto the field while the proceedings were taking place to tell me to come off immediately as Hibs didn't have clearance from the SFA for me to have played in any of the games, and in any case, by accepting the insurance payout I had effectively barred myself permanently from the professional game. I later discovered that I could play on if I wished but it would mean returning the insurance money. In the circumstances, with major doubts remaining regarding my long term fitness, I decided that it just wasn't worth the risk. I had played only on the promise of expenses, but it turned out that I didn't see any of that either, and it was back to square one.

With little money to improve the first team squad Pat Stanton had been operating with both hands tied behind his back. In difficult circumstances he had tried his best, bringing through several promising young players who would stand the club in good stead in the future, but disillusioned, Pat would soon resign from the club he had supported since a boy.

Someone had suggested that I should try the pub game, an occupation that was popular with many former players at that time. At first I wasn't all that keen, but with little else on the horizon I eventually decided to apply to all the major breweries. To improve my chances we moved back to Edinburgh and, to gain experience of the bar trade, I worked with my former coach at Hibs, John Fraser, who then ran the Learig pub in Restalrig, while Pat worked at Erich Schaedler's bar at the foot of Easter Road. I was soon offered the Phoenix Bar in Broughton Street but felt that it was too far off the beaten track and eventually settled for the Iona Bar in Easter Road which was situated just a few hundred yards from the Hibs Easter Road stadium. When I was at Arsenal a lad called Eddie Campbell who ran an amateur football club in Edinburgh had contacted me to ask for permission to call the team Liberton Cropley. I considered it a great honour and of course agreed. Now with me back in Edinburgh, Eddie went a step further and invited me to play for the team. After travelling through to Glasgow to convince a panel that my legs could not stand up to the vigour's of the professional game, I was reinstated to the amateur ranks. I enjoyed playing again, as usual taking it all very seriously, even getting upset if substituted, but in the end with my lack of fitness, the home games taking place well outside the city, and running the pub full-time, it all became too much and I was forced to pack in half way through the season. They were a great bunch of lads though and they would still regularly use the pub before and after games.

One evening a few years before when I was still with the Villa, I had been introduced at Andy Gray's nightclub the Holy City Zoo, to a girl called Elizabeth Greenan who hailed from Edinburgh but was then living in Birmingham. Now on a night out with the lads, by pure coincidence, I bumped into her again in an Edinburgh pub. It turned out that she was now back living in Scotland. By that time Pat and I were growing further and further apart and she eventually decided to move out and live in Glasgow with my son Ross. Elizabeth, her sister Maureen and pal Davina, who all had experience in the bar trade agreed to help me get the pub up and running. After a few months Devina left but Elizabeth and Maureen remained behind. The rest is history and Elizabeth and I were married in 1985. The only thing I regret is that I wish I had met her right from the very start, but in saying that, because of the person I was at that time I probably wouldn't have realised or appreciated just what I had. We now have two lovely children, Natasha who was born in 1987 and Jordan who was born two years later. My other son Ross now lives in England but phones me every week as well as the occasional visit to Edinburgh. All three of the kids get on well with each other and I am more contented now than I have ever been in my life.

But back to the pub. At that time Sky were beginning to cover live matches on TV but only for viewers in England. The former Hearts player Jim Jefferies who lived in Lauder near the border and could receive the Sky games so he would tape them for me and I would drive down to Lauder in the afternoon to collect the tapes, the game shown later that evening in the Iona Bar to appreciative customers.

Unfortunately by that time most of the other pubs in the area were well established and being the newest kids on the block we found it hard going. On match days and weekends things were great but during the week business was slack and we struggled. Looking back now, I didn't have the personality for the pub game. I was far too quiet. Supporters would come in wanting to talk football but I would prefer to sit at the end of the bar on my own. In contrast Liz was a bubbly personality ideal for the pub game, and although she didn't suffer fools gladly she got on well with most of the customers. Another major problem was the beer. Drybroughs was not overly popular with the punters. As part of the franchise I was allowed to stock the more popular Tennents in small bottles but I soon started to bring in the larger pint sized bottles which sold like hot cakes. One day the rep from Drybrough's turned up unexpectedly to examine a damaged cask and was obviously not pleased to see a Tennents lorry and trailer unloading 144 cases of bottled beer. I was immediately called up to headquarters, and as I expected my agreement was cancelled on the spot, which to be honest was something of a relief.

Through a friend of Elizabeth's I then got a job with an insurance company cold calling around the doors. If I thought I was unsuitable for the pub trade I was even worse at the insurance game and quit after only one night.

Someone then suggested that I try driving a taxi. With all due respect I didn't fancy it, but after encouragement from Elizabeth and my mum and dad, I gave it a try and passed my test at the first attempt. After a couple of years driving four nights a week for someone else, I eventually bought my own taxi, and 23 years later I still love the job. Every day is different and you meet a lot of interesting people, although a friend of mine recently told me that I must be insane if I enjoyed driving in Edinburgh with its countless roadwork's and possibly the largest number of traffic lights per head in the entire country.

In some ways professional sport can be a lonely life with very few real friends outside the game. When I left football most of my pals were still in England and the players I had known at Easter Road had now moved on. But thanks to my brother-in-law Ronnie Tolmie, who was once on the books at Celtic, I was introduced to a group of his friends for golf and was made very welcome.

There is one other person that I would particularly like to mention and that is my great friend Mike Collins. I first met Mike when he and his wife Cathie joined us and another couple on a night out. We immediately got on well together, and Mike being Mike decided that he would become my best friend, and he has been ever since. He has travelled all over the country to watch me play, Wembley, Old Trafford, Sheffield, you name it, even all the way down to Portsmouth for my testimonial game, and once when my car broke down at Southwaite Service Station, he not only drove all the way down to collect me, but also made sure that the car was collected and repaired. He is a great guy who has always been there for me, and I cannot thank him enough for his support throughout the past 40 years.

Today I am a member of both the Aston Villa and Hibernian Former Players Associations but have to say that I have little interest in attending matches, even though tickets are usually available. The football that we are seeing at Easter Road at the moment doesn't make me want to attend games. The last good side we had was under Tony Mowbray, good individuals with good skill. That's what it's all about – enjoyment and entertainment – good to watch and not just about winning. Of the present crop Alex Harris excites me. He has a good left foot and I see a lot of myself in him. With a good left foot you always have a chance. I prefer instead to spend my Saturdays either working or watching my son Jordan playing.

As youngsters both Jordan and his cousin Blair Tolmie played for the Leith Athletic Under 11's side. When they eventually moved up to the Under 13's, I was invited to coach the team. Although we had some quite good players some of them couldn't even kick the ball straight and we struggled that first season. The next year was better, and by the third they had won the Scottish Cup, all the players eventually invited to join the Hibs initiative. In time both Jordan and Blair would sign pro forms for Hibs but unfortunately both were later released. Jordan knew he was a good player as did others, but his problem was that he lacked the necessary commitment. Like me he too has a good left foot, and as I say with that you always have a chance. At the time of writing he is a plumber during the week and playing for the junior side Newtongrange Star on a Saturday. I don't think he will go any higher now but as long as he is enjoying himself that is all that matters. The same goes for my daughter Natasha who works as a receptionist for the well-known Charlie Miller's hairdresser chain and is extremely happy. Like Jordan, Natasha was very athletic as a youngster, particularly good at basketball but unfortunately she didn't keep it up. At the time of writing they both still live at home but Elizabeth and I have not entirely given up hope that someone will come along soon and take them off our hands!

In the book I have spent quite a lot of time discussing Eddie Turnbull, and I make no apologies. Quite simply Eddie Turnbull was a genius, certainly the best by far that I ever came across. He was sometimes lacking in man management, although after a particularly good victory he would always be waiting at the dressing room door to congratulate each one of us individually. There were rarely huge compliments bandied about by Eddie but I think that was because he took it for granted just how good we were, or rather how good he had made us. He was a great talker, a quite unbelievable tactician and trainer, and he made a great impression on all of us, although in saying that he was preaching to the converted. He was certainly a man well before his time, and I sometimes wonder how he would have fared in today's game. Would the players actually understand what he was talking about or even bother to take it in?

I have no real regrets regarding my career as a professional football player except for the fact that I had to retire so early because of injury. The one thing that does upset me however is when people say that I was injury prone. All my injuries were the direct result of heavy and at times badly mistimed tackles. I was not one to suffer easily from minor knocks and were it not for the bad injuries, particularly the leg breaks, I am convinced that I could well have played until I was at least 36.

There is perhaps one small thing that I would have liked to have changed. People keep telling me that I was some player, something I took in my stride and I only wish that I had really appreciated how good I apparently was at the time.

However the main thing is that I had a ball, and looking back I enjoyed every single minute of it. I have travelled the world, met some really nice people, and was paid for it. I also achieved every schoolboy's dream of playing for the team they supported, and there are not too many people who played down the park at Portobello on a Sunday morning that went on to play for their country.

CHAPTER FIFTEEN

The Last Word

SINCE WRITING THE original text for this book, Aston Villa have been relegated from the Premier League. I don't suppose that it would have been a huge surprise to many as it has been coming for some time. You just can't keep selling your best players and still expect to survive, particularly in the Premier League. Four managers in as many years, Remi Garde lasting just five months, perhaps says it all. The job has become a poisoned chalice.

I still keep an eye out for all my old sides and it was painful to watch the slow demise of a side that meant so much to me and where I shared so many happy times with a wonderful group of players.

In my opinion, Villa will struggle in the lower divisions. It all depends on who they get in as their next manager but it will be very difficult to attract a really top man. Even the likes of Moyes, Kean, Pearson or McClaren would probably turn the job down as anyone with ambition would not be keen to manage in the championship.

I really enjoyed my time at Villa Park and have nothing but fantastic memories, particularly winning the League Cup. I still keep in touch with a couple of the players including Gordon Cowans who runs the under-21 side. Gordon has not said as much but having experienced better days at Villa Park, he is probably scathing of how things have been allowed to deteriorate so rapidly.

I have an open invitation to visit on a match day from Ken McNaught who runs the Former Players Association, and my wife Liz and I have been down a few times. We are always made extremely welcome and it is great to meet up again with some of the lads. Pat Ward, Gordon Cowans, Nigel Spinks, Tony Morley, Sean Teal, Colin Gibson and some of the others still meet regularly for lunch on a match day and it is always great to reminisce about the old days.

Villa Park itself, however, is much changed from my day. The stands are much bigger, the traditional Holte End extended and now all seated, and the hospitality suites, nowadays such an important source of revenue for a club, run the entire length of the main stand.

Villa were always a fantastic family club with a great potential and a tremendous support. The last time I was down, even in the current circumstances, they were still able to attract a crowd of over 28,000 – that was for a game against Norwich City who didn't bring all that many – and on a good day are still capable of drawing crowds of around 40,000.

Perhaps what they need is a new owner, someone who is really interested in the club, but even then I am afraid that the next few years will be difficult for them.

I enjoy watching Arsenal on TV. For me they try to play the right way but at times lack a cutting edge. I can well understand the fans' frustration with Arsene Wenger, but maybe he deserves another couple of years after what he has done for the club, or at least to see the final year of his contract out – but in saying that, it is well known that there is no loyalty in football. What can't be denied, however, is that Arsenal should have won far more than two FA Cups in the past ten years. It is not nearly good enough for a club of their stature to merely be content with a place in the top four each season and qualification for the Champions League. Even managing to finish second last season for the first time in eleven years was courtesy of Spurs freak 5-1 defeat by already-relegated Newcastle United on the last day of the season.

The problem, as with most of the top sides is that if Wenger went, then who would they get to replace him as manager? Possibly there would be a place on the board for him, although he is a proud man and I am not sure that he would accept the position and would probably just walk away, similar to Alex Ferguson at Manchester United. After Matt Busby retired at Manchester United he was at the ground most days, the players still addressing him as 'boss' and this obviously seemed to create problems for several of the managers coming after him, so Wenger's hanging around would possibly be a distraction for anyone taking over from him.

On the field, however, some of Arsenal's leading up play is brilliant to watch, particularly Alexis who has proved to be an inspired signing, but for me their problems lie further back. Like all the top sides they have a very good goalkeeper in Petr Cech who really impresses me. They all impress me collectively, but for some reason they often struggle to get over the winning line. I quite like the right back Hector Bellerin who is very pacey. Left back Kieran Gibbs is perhaps not the best although he too is very fast, but I am not convinced about the centre back pairing of Laurent Koscielny and Per Mertesacker. Koscielny is not bad, but the German Mertesacker, whilst fine on the ground, lacks pace and is not all that good in the air for a man his size.

For some reason they always seems to fall at the final hurdle, guilty of trying to walk the ball into the net. Perhaps what they need is a Viera, a Roy Kean, a Souness or even a Rioch to drive them on from midfield.

Nowadays I don't have contact with anyone from Arsenal. A few years ago I was invited down to the capital by the London branch of the Hibernian supporters club for their annual Burns supper. While in London we took the opportunity to visit the Emirates and we happened to bump into my old pal Eddie Kelly who showed me around the ground. I didn't recognise Eddie at first although it has been quite a few years, so maybe he could say the same thing about me. Both Eddie and Charlie George now do the match day hospitality at Arsenal. It was the first time I had visited the Emirates and thought the stadium, which is capable of holding over 60,000 fans, is absolutely fantastic and a far cry to the Highbury where I served my time.

Nowadays I don't manage to get along to many Hibs games as I go to watch my son Jordan playing on a Saturday, although I have recently managed the occasional midweek game.

I quite like what I see at Easter Road. The team tries to play the right way, although, like Arsenal, they often have no cutting edge and usually end up trying to walk the ball into the net. They did well earlier in the season when teams were possibly a bit unsure of them, but now the other sides seem to know how to play against them and they have struggled a bit recently, although in saying that, they have still managed to reach two cup finals so they must be doing something right. However, failure to achieve promotion through the play-offs for a second consecutive season could well have been a huge financial blow to the club and could have a huge bearing on the players they bring in. The Scottish Cup final win against Rangers, however, has gone a long way towards salvaging what could well have been a dreadfully disappointing season. The victory will have been a huge boost to the supporters and will guarantee, particularly after the European football this summer, a big increase in the number of season tickets sold, although in saying that the priority for a club the size of Hibs must be to get back into the top league.

For me Hibs don't have anyone capable of going past players and they lack a physical presence in the opposition box. Also at times I don't think that they defend properly. The centre backs are not all that tall and while very good on the ground they often just manage to get away with it in the air.

Cummings disappoints me. Although he has scored a lot of goals, the penalty miss against Dundee United in the semi-final of the cup at Hampden, when he tried to be clever in chipping the goalkeeper only to send the ball over the bar, was typical of him. For me he plays for himself and not the team. Young McGinn looks a real prospect but flits in and out of a game. When I played, Pat Stanton would stamp his authority on the proceedings, bombing forward at every opportunity, although I don't suppose I am doing the young lad any favours in comparing him to such a legendary figure as Stanton, particularly at this early stage in his career.

I suppose the game has changed but surely it is still all about taking teams on on the flanks and scoring goals.

Alan Stubbs has probably proved himself as a new manager but he will possibly have to change his philosophy if he wants to go a lot further in the game. With Stubbs agreeing to a move to Rotherham, everything now depends on who Hibs bring in as the next manager. As they have already proved this season that they are more than capable of beating teams from the premiership who come at them, but championship sides now know how to play against them, often packing their defence, making it extremely difficult for the front men.

In my opinion, football in Scotland is dying a death. With attendances in general well down there is not enough money in the game. It also lacks players with personality and panache, someone who the crowds would pay good money to see. In my time most of the sides had a couple of personality players who had a bit of flair about them, but nowadays it seems to be more about not conceding goals than scoring them.

At the time of writing Rangers have just been promoted to the Premiership. They will eventually do well but it might take them a couple of years. It all depends on how much money Dave King is willing to plough in.

As for myself I can still be found driving my taxi around Edinburgh, although I have to say that the city is getting worse. Everywhere you go there are traffic lights, pedestrian lights, road works and no entry signs. A few years ago I would sometimes get a bit of grief from customers, often good naturedly from Hearts fans, the Hibs supporters keen to talk to me about the game, but with the passing of the years nobody knows me nowadays, even some of the neighbours where I live. Occasionally I will see someone looking, wondering – 'is it, or is not?' – but they rarely come up and speak.

Recently a group of former players were invited down to Easter Road for lunch and it was great to catch up and talk about the old days. I took the opportunity to go trackside that afternoon and I have to admit that the memories came flooding back. Although the ground, including the pitch which has now had the famous slope removed, is far different to what I remember, I could still visualise many of the games and the goals, particularly the electric atmosphere of the European games.

Unlike many former professionals, I didn't miss the game or the dressing room banter when I first retired from playing. I knew it was time to leave. I wasn't fit and was well aware that it was impossible for me to continue. I was finding something that used to come so easy to me becoming harder and harder, and although I was still only 31 it was obvious that it was time for me to go.

For some reason that afternoon at pitch side was different, very emotional. I could almost hear the crowds roaring me on and for a moment wished that I was back playing again.

However, you can't turn the clock back, but I can honestly say that I had a ball and would not have missed any of it for the world.

My Greatest Team

I HAVE BEEN asked to put together my best side from players that I have played alongside. This as you can no doubt imagine has been an extremely difficult, and in some cases almost impossible task, and I apologise to many of the great players that I have had to leave out. I have not included myself, not through any sense of false modesty, but purely because I would have struggled to get a game, even as a substitute. In 4-3-3 formation I would have to select:

BOBBY CLARK
(ABERDEEN)

JOHN BROWNLIE   MARTIN BUCHAN   JOHN BLACKLEY   JOHN ROBSON
(HIBERNIAN)   (ABERDEEN AND SCOTLAND)   (HIBERNIAN)   (ASTON VILLA)

ALAN BALL   PAT STANTON   LIAM BRADY
(ARSENAL)   (HIBERNIAN)   (ARSENAL)

JIMMY JOHNSTONE   ANDY GRAY   GORDON COWANS
(CELTIC)   (ASTON VILLA)   (ASTON VILLA)

SUBS:
JIMMY RIMMER (ARSENAL AND ASTON VILLA)
JOHN O'HARE (DERBY COUNTY AND SCOTLAND)
BILLY BREMNER (LEEDS UNITED AND SCOTLAND)
BRIAN LITTLE (ASTON VILLA)

MANAGER: ONLY ONE NAME IN THE FRAME BY A MILE AND THAT IS EDDIE TURNBULL
OF HIBERNIAN.
TRAINER AND PHYSIO: AGAIN ONLY ONE PERSON FOR CONSIDERATION –
TOM MCNIVEN OF HIBERNIAN.

Alex Cropley
Team Appearances

Senior Career

	Club	Appearances	Goals
1968–74	Hibernian	118	27
1974–76	Arsenal	30	5
1976–80	Aston Villa	67	7
1979–80	Newcastle United (loan)	3	0
1981	Toronto Blizzard	15	2
1981–82	Portsmouth	10	2
Total		228	41

(Senior club appearances and goals counted for UK matches only.)

International Caps

1971	Scotland v Portugal	Euro '72 qualifiers	2-1
1971	Scotland v Belgium	Euro '72 qualifiers	1-0

Definitely the Last Word

THE EARLY '70S WAS a great time to be at Easter Road. The team was packed full of fantastic players each with his own particular talents, but my favourite was always Alex Cropley. With his educated left foot, Alex was a tremendous talent, but I have to say he could also be a real pain in the neck. A nippy sweetie, he was always moaning, but that is often the sign of a great player – a real determination to succeed and a refusal to settle for second best.

He was some player though, exciting, and terrific to play alongside. Although he was not the biggest in stature, he was frightened of nobody and tackled like a full back. There are some tackles that you should not go anywhere near, but this never put Alex off. He was utterly fearless, shirked nothing and was a great favourite with the fans.

Because of his lack of inches he was not the greatest in the air but he always made sure that the defender didn't get a good header in.

He could play wide on the left but his best position was in the centre of the park where he could use his outstanding football brain to set up moves for others. Not everyone can play in midfield but he linked up well, usually with me and Alex Edwards. He had a great left foot, great vision, was quick in thought and action, and knew exactly how to use his pace and when to make his runs.

Unfortunately injury prevented him from adding to his total of international caps, but it was obvious to me that, even at an early age, he was destined for a move to England in the near future.

I consider myself lucky to have got a close up view of an outstanding player. I was always impressed, and it was a privilege to play alongside him for both Hibs and Scotland.

Pat Stanton

Some other books published by **Luath Press**

Hibernian: From Joe Baker to Turnbull's Tornadoes
Tom Wright

ISBN 978 1908873 09 1 HBK £20

In *Hibernian: From Joe Baker to Turnbull's Tornadoes*, club historian Tom Wright marks a new dawn for the game and the end of an era for Hibs.

Hibernian begins in the turbulent 1960s, when relegation was avoided at Easter Road on the final day of the 1963 season.

The appointment of the legendary manager Jock Stein in 1964 saw an immediate improvement in the relegation haunted side. The Hibs side of the mid-'60s featured an all-Scottish international forward line, and the return of player Eddie Turnbull in 1971 saw the emergence of possibly Hibs' greatest-ever side – the magical Turnbull's Tornadoes.

Packed full of detail and interesting information, Hibernian is a must not only for Hibs supporters, but also for the general football fan who is interested in this defining period in the history of our game.

We Are Hibernian: Scottish Cup Winners 2016
Andy MacVannan
ISBN 978-1-910745-70-0 HBK £14.99

We are Hibernian explores the sights, sounds and memories of fans who have taken the 'journey' to watch the team that they love. Supporters from all walks of life bare their souls with humour, emotion and sincerity.

Featuring interviews with many different fans, this book takes you on a journey to discover why football is more than just a game and why Hibernian is woven into the DNA of each and every one of its supporters.

The Scottish Cup 2016 edition contains new material celebrates Hibernian's historic triumph.

It was a huge feeling of relief when the final whistle went, but it was also very emotional as well. A lot of people round about me were in tears and were absolutely overwhelmed.
MICKY WEIR, FORMER PLAYER

Walking away from that cup final I said, 'The club will survive now.'
CHARLIE REID, MUSICIAN

Everyone walked out that ground like they had just seen the second coming.
IRVINE WELSH, WRITER

In the early 1950s Alan, Dougie and I caught the tail end of the legendary Hibs team when they were still the best team in the world.
BRUCE FINDLAY, MUSIC BUSINESS MANAGER

Stramash: Tackling Scotland's Towns and Teams
Daniel Gray

ISBN 978 1906817 66 4 PBK £9.99

Fatigued by bloated big-time football and bored of samey big cities, Daniel Gray went in search of small town Scotland and its teams. Part travelogue, part history, and part mistakenly spilling ketchup on the face of a small child, Stramash takes an uplifting look at the country's nether regions.

Using the excuse of a match to visit places from Dumfries to Dingwall, *Stramash* accomplishes the feats of visiting Dumfries without mentioning Robert Burns, being positive about Cumbernauld and linking Elgin City to Lenin. It is ae fond look at Scotland as you've never seen it before.

... a must-read for every non-Old Firm football fan – and for many Rangers and Celtic supporters too.
DAILY RECORD

There have been previous attempts by authors to explore the off-the-beaten paths of the Scottish football landscape, but Daniel Gray's volume is in another league.
THE SCOTSMAN

A brilliant way to rediscover Scotland.
THE HERALD

I defy anyone to read Stramash *and not fall in love with Scottish football's blessed eccentricities all over again... Funny enough to bring on involuntary, laugh out loud moments.*
THE SCOTTISH FOOTBALL BLOG

Details of books published by Luath Press can be found at:
www.luath.co.uk

Luath Press Limited

committed to publishing well written books worth reading

LUATH PRESS takes its name from Robert Burns, whose little collie
Luath (*Gael.*, swift or nimble) tripped up Jean Armour at a wedding
and gave him the chance to speak to the woman who was to be his wife
and the abiding love of his life. Burns called one of the 'Twa Dogs'
Luath after Cuchullin's hunting dog in Ossian's *Fingal*.
Luath Press was established in 1981 in the heart of
Burns country, and is now based a few steps up
the road from Burns' first lodgings on
Edinburgh's Royal Mile. Luath offers you
distinctive writing with a hint of
unexpected pleasures.
Most bookshops in the UK, the US, Canada,
Australia, New Zealand and parts of Europe,
either carry our books in stock or can order them
for you. To order direct from us, please send a £sterling
cheque, postal order, international money order or your
credit card details (number, address of cardholder and
expiry date) to us at the address below. Please add post
and packing as follows: UK – £1.00 per delivery address;
overseas surface mail – £2.50 per delivery address; overseas airmail –
£3.50 for the first book to each delivery address, plus £1.00 for each
additional book by airmail to the same address. If your order is a gift,
we will happily enclose your card or message at no extra charge.

Luath Press Limited
543/2 Castlehill
The Royal Mile
Edinburgh EH1 2ND
Scotland
Telephone: +44 (0)131 225 4326 (24 hours)
Email: sales@luath. co.uk
Website: www. luath.co.uk